aventura

LIBRO DEL ALUMNO

Rosa María Martín

Martyn Ellis

Hodder & Stoughton

A MEMBER OF THE HODDER HEADLINE GROUP

Acknowledgements

The authors would like to thank the following people for their contribution to the production of this book:

Tessa and Isabel Ellis, our daughters; the Señores Manuel Martín and Rosa Yuste; the children of Belchite and Zaragoza who allowed themselves to be photographed and recorded; the director, staff and children of Colegio Belia, Belchite; the director and staff of the Centro Cultural Delicias, Club A Dalla and Club Musaraña in Zaragoza, and of the summer camp in Broto; children from Broomfield School, Enfield and the Spanish School in Wood Green, London; all the friends and relations who allowed us to photograph the interiors of their houses, their vehicles, taxis, shops, businesses and themselves; Gerald Ramshaw and Franco Capone for sound and songs; Marina Barrull for the extra activities; and finally the team at Hodder, Annette Love, Helen Parker and Tim Gregson-Williams; not forgetting everyone else who has contributed to this book.

The authors and publishers are grateful to the following for permission to reproduce photographs:

Dan Addelman p.128; A.G.E. Fotostock p.141; Associated Press/Topham p.99; Colorsport p.99; Departamento de Comerç, Consum i Turisme de la Generalitat de Catalunya pp.42, 105, 111; Lorraine Inglis p.129; Barbara Ingram-Monk pp.105, 129; John Birdsall Photography p.43; Life File pp.23, 42, 45, 89, 91, 129, 139; Helen Parker pp.62, 70; David Phillips p.128; Janet Ravenscroft p.38; Robert Harding Picture Library, photographer: Ken Gilham p.141.

The authors and publishers would like to thank the following for permission to reproduce copyright material in this volume:

Photograph © 1994, The Art Institute of Chicago, All Rights Reserved: Salvador Dalí, Spanish, 1904-1989, Mae West, gouache over photographic print, c.1934, 8.3 x 17.8 cm, Gift of Mrs. Gilbert W. Chapman in memory of Charles B. Goodspeed, 1949.517 and © DEMART PRO ARTE BV/DACS 1995 p.119; Ayuntamiento de Zaragoza and Brut de diseño p.141; Centro de Información y Promoción de Actividades Juveniles p.80; Cooperativa Auto-Taxis, Zaragoza p.18; Decoración Vanidades, Editorial América, S.A. p.119; Editorial Andina, S.A. p.53; El Corte Inglés, S.A. p.99; Fundació Barcelona Olímpico pp.84, 85, 99; Guarro Casas, S/A p.26; McDonald's Sistemas de España, Inc. p.70; MÍA Cocina No 3 p.75; Naipes Heraclio Fournier, S.A. p.19; © 1995 Société des Produits Nestlé S.A., 1800 Vevey, Switzerland, Trademark Owners and Nestlé España S.A., 8950 Esplugues de Llobregat, Spain p.93; Organización Nacional de Ciegos p.18; Organismo Nacional de Loterías y Apuestos del Estado p.18; Santanilla, S.A. p.133; Suplemento Semanal, El País Internacional, S.A. p.99; Toys 'Я' Us Iberia S.A. p.63.

The publishers would like to thank the following for use of their material:

Ayuntamiento de Belchite p.140; Chica Hoy CIBRA, S.A. p.89; Coktel Educative Multimedia, S.L. p.81; Ediciones Sicilia p.103; Furia Musical p.39; GENTE CE p.59; La Vanguardia, Cataluña Universal p.111; Superpop p.75; Suplemento Semanal p.37; Tiempo p.85.

The authors and publishers would also like to thank the following for their illustrations: Phil Dobson, Richard Duszczak, David Farris, Sascha Lipscombe, Derek Mathews, Fred Pipes, Venice Shone, Jane Smith and Andrew Warrington.

Design concept and cover illustration: Amanda Hawkes
Design: Mind's Eye Design, Lewes.

The authors and publishers have made every possible effort to trace all copyright holders. In the few cases where copyright holders could not be traced, due acknowledgement will be given in future reprintings if copyright holders make themselves known to the publishers.

British Library Cataloging-in-Publication Data

ISBN 0-340-63100-7

Martín, Rosa María
Aventura. - Book 1
I. Title II. Ellis, Martyn
468.3421

First published 1995
Impression number 10 9 8 7 6 5 4
Year   2002 2001 2000 1999

Printed in Great Britain for Hodder and Stoughton Educational, a division of Hodder Headline Plc, 338 Euston Road, London, NW1 3BH, by Scotprint, Musselburgh, Scotland.

Contents

Contents

¡Bienvenidos a aventura!

Welcome to **aventura**, a course that will help you to learn Spanish and to have fun at the same time! In Spanish there are quite a few words that are similar to English so you will find that you can understand and use lots of new words very quickly. We hope you find Spanish an exciting and interesting language to learn. It can be hard work, but if you make up your mind you are going to enjoy yourself, then it will be great fun too!

Here are some hints to help you get the most from **aventura** ...

- In class, try to speak Spanish at all times. Try things out, even if you are not sure of the words. You will soon find that you can make sentences which people understand. Don't be afraid of making mistakes. If you help each other, you will soon find that you can understand each other in a new language!

- Use the vocabulary section at the back of the book to look up words you don't know. All the words in this book are there. If you can't find a word then try a bigger dictionary.

- Use the grammar section to find explanations of the way Spanish sentences are made and to practise the patterns of the different kinds of verbs.

- Make sure you do all your homework and practise the new words and sentences you have learnt.

- Most important of all, enjoy yourself.

Good luck!   ¡Buena suerte!

SYMBOLS IN aventura

There are symbols to help you understand what kind of activity you are doing. The main ones are given here and are usually followed by more instructions in Spanish.

 Listening

 Speaking

 Reading

 Writing

OTHER SYMBOLS THAT APPEAR

 Tells you that you may need to look up words.

 Reminds you not to write in this book.

 Reminds you to look at the grammar section for more help.

 Helps you with vocabulary.

Main instructions for tasks

The instructions to the tasks in **aventura** are all in Spanish. Next to each symbol you will see more detailed instructions for each task in Spanish:

 Escucha ...

 Habla ...

 Lee ...

 Escribe ...

You will often see these instructions in combination with others. Here are some examples:

Escucha y repite.
Escucha y comprueba.
Escucha y completa el cuadro.
Escucha e indica.

Listen and repeat.
Listen and check your answer.
Listen and complete the grid.
Listen and indicate.

Lee la carta.
Lee el artículo.
Lee y ordena el diálogo.

Read the letter.
Read the article.
Read and order the dialogue.

Habla con tu compañero(a).
Pregunta a tus compañeros(as).
Encuesta de la clase.

Speak with your classmate.
Ask your classmates.
Class survey.

Escribe una lista.
Escribe la información.
Escribe frases.

Write a list.
Write the information.
Write sentences.

Main instructions for tasks

You will also see these phrases:

Adivina (Adivinad)	*Guess*
Ahora tú	*Now you*
Busca	*Look for*
Canta	*Sing*
Cambia	*Change*
Comprueba	*Check*
Completa	*Complete*
Contesta	*Answer*
Continúa	*Continue the task*
Describe	*Describe*
Dibuja	*Draw*
Dicta	*Dictate*
Ejemplo	*Example*
Elige	*Choose*
Estudia	*Study*
Indica	*Indicate, mark*
Inventa	*Invent*
Lee en voz alta	*Read aloud*
Mira	*Look*
Prepara un póster	*Prepare a poster*
Une	*Link, join*
¿Verdad o mentira?	*True or false?*

Here are some more examples:

Adopta una personalidad.	*Adopt a personality.*
Busca las nuevas palabras en el vocabulario.	*Look up new words in the vocabulary.*
Canta la canción.	*Sing the song.*
Completa el cuadro.	*Complete the grid.*
Completa la información.	*Complete the information.*
Dicta tu número de teléfono.	*Dictate your phone number.*
Une las palabras con los dibujos.	*Link words with the drawings.*

General classroom language

You will hear from your teacher:

Abre (Abrid) el libro.	*Open your books.*
Aprended de memoria.	*Learn off by heart.*
Cierra (Cerrad) el libro.	*Close your books.*
Coge el bolígrafo.	*Pick up your pen.*
Cuando termines (terminéis).	*When you finish.*
¿Cuántos puntos tienes?	*How many marks have you got? (to one person)*
¿Cuántos puntos tenéis?	*How many marks have you got? (to the group)*
Dame el cuaderno.	*Give me your exercise book.*
Dime (Decidme).	*Tell me.*
Empieza (Empezad).	*Begin.*
En casa.	*At home.*
En silencio.	*In silence.*
Encuentra (Encontrad).	*Find.*
Escucha (Escuchad) el cassette.	*Listen to the cassette.*
Escucha (Escuchad) la cinta.	*Listen to the tape.*
Espera (Esperad).	*Wait.*
Excelente.	*Excellent.*

Habla (Hablad) en español.	*Speak in Spanish.*
¿Has (Habéis) terminado?	*Have you finished?*
Haz el ejercicio/la actividad/el test.	*Do the exercise/activity/test.*
Individualmente.	*On your own.*
Levantaos.	*Stand up (to the group).*
Levántate.	*Stand up (to one person).*
Marca ✔ en la casilla.	*Put a tick in the box.*
Marca ✘ en la casilla.	*Put a cross in the box.*
Mima (Mimad).	*Mime.*
Mira (Mirad) el diccionario.	*Look in the dictionary.*
Muy bien.	*Very good.*
No está bien.	*It's not very good.*
No mires (miréis).	*Don't look.*
Otra vez.	*(Try) again.*
Pon (Poned).	*Place, put.*

Por favor.	Please.
¿Qué dice?	What is he/she saying?
¿Qué dicen?	What are they saying?
Repasa (Repasad).	Revise.
¿Sabes (Sabéis)?	Do you know?
Sentaos.	Sit down (to the group).
Siéntate.	Sit down (to one person).
Silencio.	Silence.
Sin diccionario.	Without the dictionary.
Termina (Terminad).	Stop.
¿Tienes los deberes?	Do you have your homework?
Toma el bolígrafo.	Take your pen.
Trabajad en grupos.	Work in groups.
Trabajad en pares.	Work in pairs.
Vamos a cantar.	We are going to sing.
Vamos a jugar.	We are going to play.
Voy a pasar lista.	I'm going to call the register.
¿Ya está?	Is it ready?

You will need to say:

Can you repeat please?	Repite (Repita), por favor.
How do you say cat in Spanish?	¿Cómo se dice cat en español?
How is it spelt?	¿Cómo se escribe?
I'm sorry I'm late.	Siento llegar tarde.
I'm sorry.	Lo siento.
I'm sorry.	Perdona (Perdone).
I don't have a pen.	No tengo bolígrafo.
I don't understand.	No entiendo.
I don't understand	No comprendo.
It's my turn.	Me toca a mí.
Just a moment, please.	Un momento, por favor.
Slower, please.	Más despacio, por favor.
What did you say?	¿Qué dices?.
Your turn.	Ahora tú.
Your turn.	Te toca.

Mapa del mundo

OCÉANO
ÁRTICO

OCÉANO
ATLÁNTICO

Cuba

España

República
Dominicana

Puerto Rico

Panamá

los Estados Unidos

México

Guatemala

El Salvador

Honduras

Nicaragua

Costa Rica

Ecuador

Perú

Chile

Venezuela

Colombia

Bolivia

Paraguay

Uruguay

Argentina

OCÉANO
PÁCIFICO

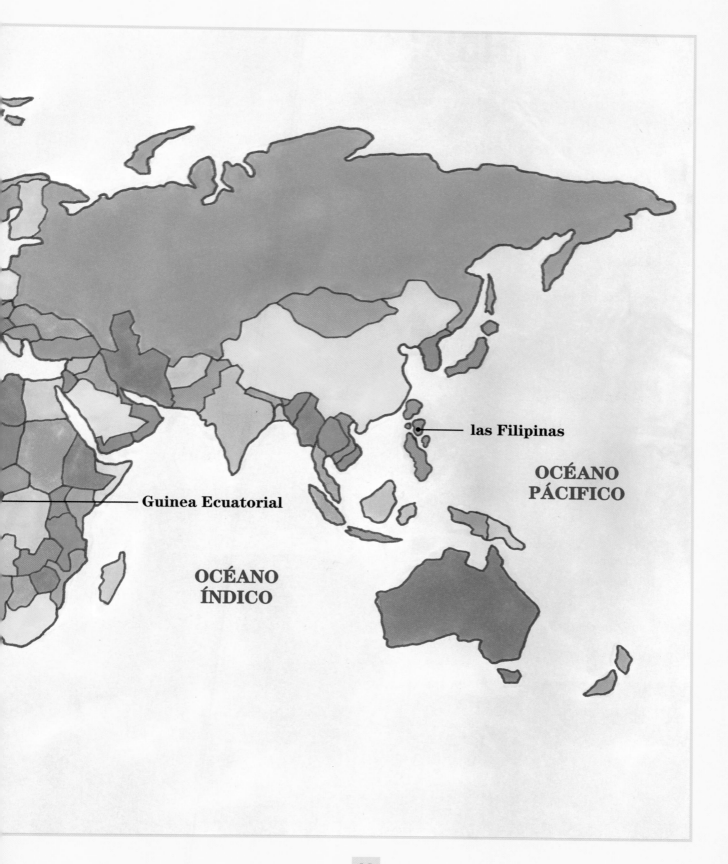

las Filipinas

OCÉANO
PÁCIFICO

Guinea Ecuatorial

OCÉANO
ÍNDICO

¡Hola!

● *Saludar y decir adiós.*

● *Presentarte y decir tu nombre.*

A ¡Hola!

1 Escucha y repite.

¡Hola!

¡Hola!

Buenos días

Buenas tardes

Buenas noches

Adiós

2 ¿Qué dicen? Habla con tu compañero(a).

Ejemplo 1 = Buenas noches

B Tu nombre

3 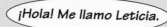 **Escucha los nombres y ordena las fotos.**

¡Hola! Me llamo Leticia.

Raúl   **Leticia**   **Tatiana**   **Tessa**   **Héctor**

1	Leticia
2	
3	
4	
5	

¡no escribas aquí!

4 **Ahora tú. Habla con tus compañeros(as).**

Ejemplo ¡Hola! Me llamo .... ¿Y tú?

5 **Escucha. Indica los nombres similares en inglés o en tu idioma.**

Juan	✔ John	Gustavo			Alejandra	
David		Sara			Isabel	
Pilar	✘	Beatriz			Ignacio	
Miguel		Teresa		¡no escribas aquí!	Carmen	
Antonio		Ana			Margarita	
Pedro		Daniel			Jaime	
María		José			Rosa	

6 **Escribe dos listas.**
¿Chicos o chicas?

Chicos
Juan
David

Chicas
Pilar

Pronunciación

Vowels in Spanish have a very short, sharp sound.
Escucha.

A	E	I	O	U
a	e	i	o	u
Ana	Elena	Isabel	Oscar	tú

a e i o u
Más sabe el burrito que tú.

7 ⟨?⟩ **Mira estos nombres. ¿Qué dibujo es? Usa el vocabulario.**

Ejemplo 1 = Mar

a Mar

b Sol

c Paloma

d Nieves

e Ángel

f Blanca

g Rosa

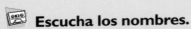 **Escucha los nombres.**

C ¿Cómo te llamas?

Escucha.

Me llamo Leticia. ¿Y tú?

¡Hola! ¿Cómo te llamas?

Me llamo Tessa.

8 Completa la información.

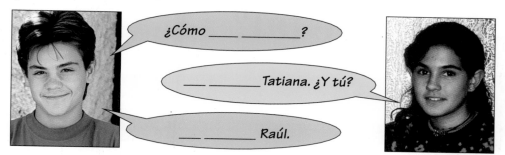

¿Cómo ___ _____?

___ _____ Tatiana. ¿Y tú?

___ _____ Raúl.

9 Ahora tú. Habla con tus compañeros(as).

10 Lee y ordena el diálogo. Ejemplo 1 = a

a ¡Hola!

b Adiós Tessa.

c Me llamo Leticia, ¿y tú?

d Adiós Leticia.

e ¡Hola! ¿Cómo te llamas?

f Me llamo Tessa.

Escucha a las chicas y comprueba.

11 ¿Cuántos nombres identificas?

Alexandra

Antonio

José

Carmen

¡Ya sabes!

¡Hola!	Buenos días
Adiós	Buenas tardes
	Buenas noches

¿Cómo te llamas? Me llamo Ana. ¿Y tú?

Nombres de chicos: Juan, David, Raúl, Miguel, José, etc.

Nombres de chicas: María, Leticia, Pilar, Ana, etc.

Aventura Semanal

¡Hola! Me llamo Ana. ¿Cómo te llamas?
¡Hola! Me llamo Ana. ¿Cómo te llamas?
¡Hola! Me llamo John. Adiós.
¡Hola! Me llamo John. Adiós.

La canción

¿Qué tal?

O B J E T I V O

● *Decir qué tal estás y preguntar a tu compañero(a).*

● *Decir cuántos años tienes y preguntar a tu compañero(a).*

A **¿Qué tal Elena?**

1   Mira y escucha.

Bien. ¿Y tú?

1

Elena

Regular.

2

Tessa

Mal.

3

Leticia

2   Escucha a los chicos y chicas e indica.

Chico(a)	Bien	Mal	Regular
1		✔	
2			
3		¡no escribas aquí!	
4			
5			

3   Mira los dibujos y completa.

¿Qué tal? _____.   ¿Qué tal? _____.   ¿Qué tal? _____.

4   Pregunta a tus compañeros(as): **¿Qué tal?**

B Los números

5 🔊 **Escucha a los chicos y chicas y repite.**

0 cero		**7** siete	
1 uno		**8** ocho	
2 dos		**9** nueve	
3 tres		**10** diez	
4 cuatro		**11** once	
5 cinco		**12** doce	
6 seis		**13** trece	

14 catorce		**17** diecisiete
15 quince		**18** dieciocho
16 dieciséis		**19** diecinueve

Pronunciación

In Spanish the letter **c** has two sounds.

In front of **e** and **i** it sounds like '**th**'.

Escucha.

cero **c**in**c**o on**c**e do**c**e tre**c**e
cator**c**e quin**c**e

In front of **a**, **u** and **o** it sounds like '**k**'.

Escucha.

cator**c**e **cu**atro **c**in**c**o

6 🔊 **Escucha a Tessa. Indica los números que *no* dice.**

0	1	(2)	3	4	5	6	7	8	9	10
11	12	13	14	15	16	17	18	19		

7 🔊 **Escucha y une los números.**

0	1	2	3	4
5	6	7	8	9
10	11	12	13	14
15	16	17	18	19

¿Qué número es?

8 🔊 **Escucha y escribe los números de teléfono.**

Ejemplo

1 682 150   **2**    **3**    **4**

✏️ **Ahora escribe los números en palabras.**
Ejemplo 1 = Seis, ocho, dos, uno, cinco, cero.

9 💬 **Ahora dicta *tu* número de teléfono a tu compañero(a).**
    Escribe el número de tu compañero(a).

10 ✎ **Escribe los números.**

Ejemplo 1 = Tres, seis, dos, nueve.

11 📼 **¿Qué número gana el premio? Escucha y comprueba.**

C ¿Cuántos años tienes?

12 📼 **Mira y escucha.**

¿Cuántos años tienes?

Tengo trece años. ¿Y tú?

Tengo once años.

13 **¿Cuántos años tienen los chicos y chicas? ¡Adivina!**

Isabel

Raúl

Jaime

Tatiana

Nombre	¿Cuántos años?	✔/ ✘
Isabel		
Raúl	¡no escribas aquí!	
Jaime		
Tatiana		

Escucha y comprueba.

14 **Pregunta a tus compañeros(as): ¿Cuántos años tienes?**

Aventura Semanal – ¿Sabes?

Las cartas españolas son diferentes. Tienen cuatro clases: Oros (12 cartas), Copas (12 cartas), Espadas (12 cartas) y Bastos (12 cartas). Son 48 cartas en total.

Oros

Copas

Espadas

Bastos

¡Ya sabes!

¿Qué tal?
Bien.
Mal.
Regular.

Los números: 0, 1, 2, …, 18, 19
Tu número de teléfono.

¿Cuántos años **tienes**?
Tengo doce años.¿Y tú?

La cartera

- *Decir qué tienes en la cartera.*
- *Preguntar a tu compañero(a).*

A La cartera

Mira y escucha.

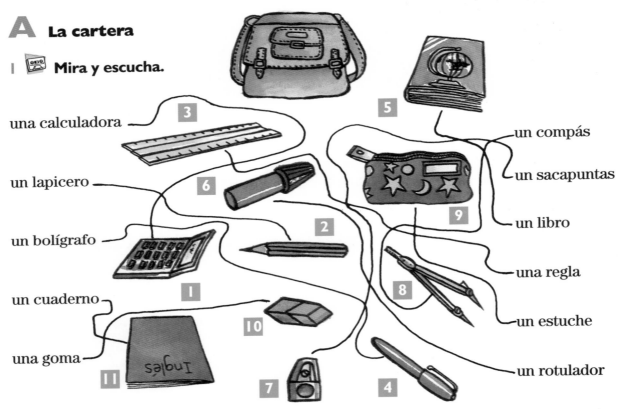

una calculadora
3
5
un compás

un lapicero
6
un sacapuntas

un bolígrafo
2
un libro

1
una regla

un cuaderno
8

una goma
9
un estuche

10

Inglés
11
7
4
un rotulador

Une las palabras con los objetos.

In Spanish names of objects ending in **o** are usually masculine.
Those that end in **a** are usually feminine.

Masculino		Femenino	
un	lapicer**o**	una	calculador**a**
un	bolígraf**o**	una	gom**a**
un	cuadern**o**	una	regl**a**

¡Nota!   un   estuch**e**

144

B ¿Tienes una goma?

2  Lee y escucha el diálogo.

3 Escucha. Indica los objetos que tienen Tessa y Raúl.

	Tessa	Raúl
un bolígrafo		
una goma	✔	✔
un estuche		
un cuaderno		
un lapicero	✗	✔
un libro		
una regla		
un sacapuntas		
un rotulador		
un compás		
una calculadora		

¡no escribas aquí!

4 Busca las diferencias.

GOM	GOMA
ESTUCHE	ESTUCH
CALCULADORA	CALCULADRA
LAPICERO	LAPICRO
RGLA	REGLA
SACAPUNTS	SACAPUNTAS
CUADERN	CUADERNO
COMPÁS	COPÁS
LIBO	LIBRO
ROTULDOR	ROTULADOR
BOLGRAFO	BOLÍGRAFO

5 Escribe una lista de las palabras correctas. ¿Un o una?

Ejemplo Un estuche

Una goma

6 Lee el diálogo.

¿Tienes una goma?

Sí.

¿Tienes un lapicero?

No, no tengo.

Ahora tú. Continúa el diálogo con tu compañero(a).

C ¿Qué tienes en la cartera?

7 ¿Qué tienes en *tu* cartera? ¿Qué tiene tu compañero(a)? Escribe dos listas.

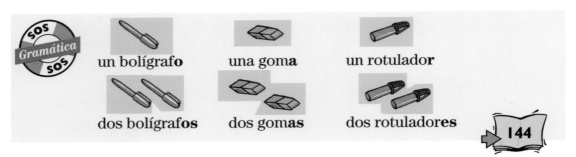

SOS *Gramática* SOS

un bolígraf**o**   una gom**a**   un rotulado**r**

dos bolígraf**os**   dos gom**as**   dos rotulado**res**

144

8 Escucha. Une la persona con la cartera.

1 Goreti

2 Cristian

3 Elena

a

b

c

9 **Mira el anuncio de cosas para el colegio.**
   Escribe dos listas, una para Ana y una para su hermano, Jorge.

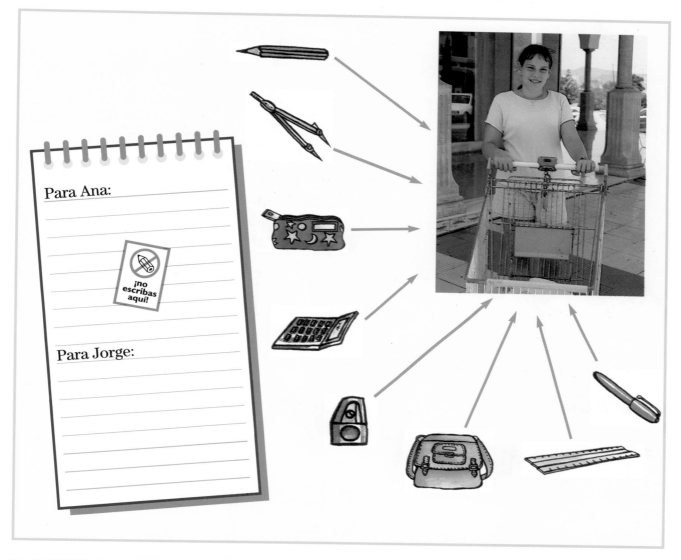

Para Ana:

¡no escribas aquí!

Para Jorge:

Aventura Semanal

¿Qué tienes en la cartera
que pesa de esta manera?
¿Qué tienes en la cartera
que pesa de esta manera?
¿Tienes una regla? Sí
¿Un rotulador? No
¿Tienes un cuaderno? Sí
¿Y los libros? No

La canción

¡Ya sabes!

¿Qué tienes en la cartera?
Tengo **dos** cuaderno**s**.

¿**Tienes** una goma?
Sí.
No, no **tengo**.

Vocabulario de la cartera: un lapicer**o**,
una gom**a**, un cuaderno, una regl**a**,
un comp**ás**, etc.

Mis asignaturas

OBJETIVO

● *Hablar de tus asignaturas.*   ● *Decir los días de la semana.*

A ¿Qué estudias?

1 Escucha y repite.

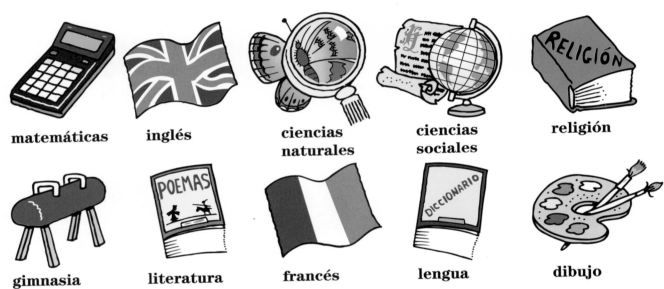

matemáticas   inglés   ciencias naturales   ciencias sociales   religión

gimnasia   literatura   francés   lengua   dibujo

2 ¿Qué asignaturas estudian los chicos? Escucha y completa.

	José	Raúl	Tatiana
matemáticas			
inglés			
ciencias naturales	✔		
ciencias sociales			
lenguaje		¡no escribas aquí!	
religión			
dibujo			
francés			✗
gimnasia			
literatura			

José

Raúl

Tatiana

3 ¿Y tú? ¿Qué asignaturas estudias?
Escribe una lista.

4 Habla con tu compañero(a).

¿Qué asignaturas estudias?

Estudio inglés y matemáticas. ¿Y tú?

Pronunciación

In Spanish **g** and **j** often have the same sound.

Escucha.

geografía **gi**mnasia reli**gi**ón dibu**jo**

g + e = **ge**ografía,
g + i = **gi**mnasia, reli**gi**ón
j + a = **Ja**ime
j + e = lengua**je**
j + o = dibu**jo**, **Jo**sé
j + u = **Ju**an

B Los días de la semana

5 Mira el calendario. Escucha.

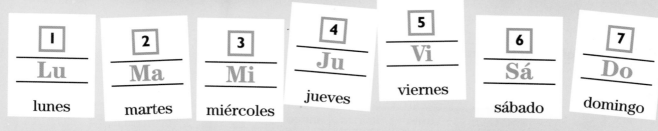

1	2	3	4	5	6	7
Lu	Ma	Mi	Ju	Vi	Sá	Do
lunes	martes	miércoles	jueves	viernes	sábado	domingo

6 Escucha. Cristian dice los días de la semana. ¿Qué día falta?

C El horario

7 Escucha el horario de Tessa y completa.

¡Atención!

el lunes = **on** Monday

el día = the day
la semana = the week
el horario = the timetable

Los días	Las asignaturas
lunes	
martes	
miércoles	 ¡no escribas aquí!
jueves	
viernes	

8 **Estudiante A: Mira el horario A.**
Estudiante B: Mira el horario B.

Habla con tu compañero(a).

¿Qué estudias el lunes?

Estudio matemáticas y francés.

Horario A

	lunes	martes	miércoles	jueves	viernes
dibujo	✔	✔		✔	✔
inglés		✔	✔	✔	✔
ciencias sociales	✔		✔	✔	

Horario B

	lunes	martes	miércoles	jueves	viernes
matemáticas	✔	✔	✔	✔	✔
francés	✔		✔	✔	✔
ciencias naturales		✔	✔		✔

9 **Completa tu horario en español.**

HORARIO	LUNES	MARTES	MIÉRCOLES	JUEVES	VIERNES	SÁBADO	DOMINGO
				¡no escribas aquí!			

10 **Busca las asignaturas en el diccionario.**

deporte   química   informática

educación física   biología   música

física   drama

D El abecedario español

11 🎵 **Escucha el abecedario y repite.**

A B C D E F G H I J K L M
N Ñ O P Q R S T U V W X Y Z

¡Ahora canta el abecedario!

12 💬 **¿Cómo se escribe tu nombre? Habla con un compañero(a).**

¡Hola! Me llamo Jaime.

¿Cómo se escribe?

J-A-I-M-E

Aventura Semanal – ¿Sabes?

En Cataluña, Euskadi (País Vasco) y Galicia, la educación es bilingüe. Los niños hablan y estudian en catalán, euskera (vasco) y gallego. Todos hablan también castellano (español).

La Coruña
GALLEGO
Bilbao
EUSKERA
CASTELLANO
Barcelona
CATALÁN
Valencia
Alicante
Sevilla

¡Ya sabes!

¿Qué **estudias**?
¿Qué asignaturas **estudias**?
Estudio matemáticas.

Las asignaturas: inglés, francés, gimnasia, biología, informática, etc.

Los días de la semana: lunes, martes, miércoles, jueves, viernes, sábado, domingo.

¿Qué estudias **el** lunes?
El lunes estudio literatura.

¡Hola! Me llamo Leticia.
¿Cómo se escribe?
L-E-T-I-C-I-A

Mi colegio

● **Decir dónde estudias.** ● **Describir tu colegio.**

A ¿Dónde estudias?

I Mira y escucha. Une el colegio con el chico o la chica.

Estudio en el colegio Belia.

el colegio Sagrado Corazón

el colegio Miraflores

el colegio La Salle Montemolín

el colegio Doctor Azúa

Leticia

Estefanía

Pili

Cristian

2 **Escribe frases. Ejemplo** Raúl: Estudio en el colegio Belia.

3 **Ahora tú. Elige un colegio y pregunta a tus compañeros(as): ¿Dónde estudias?**

B ¿Qué hay en el colegio de Raúl?

4 Mira las fotos. Escucha y repite.

5 Une las fotos con las palabras.

a el laboratorio   b la biblioteca
c el patio   d el gimnasio
e la clase   f el comedor
g la sala de vídeo

6 Habla con tus compañeros(as).
Ejemplo La foto número 3 es el laboratorio.

7 Escucha a Tessa y Raúl.

¿Qué hay en el colegio Belia?

Hay un laboratorio...

 Gramática SOS   155

Hay	**un** estudiante	Hay	estudiantes
	una clase		clases
	una biblioteca		bibliotecas

Indica lo que hay en el colegio de Raúl.

8 ✍ **Mira el plano. Leticia describe su colegio en una carta. Completa la carta.**

Querida Tessa:

Aquí hay un plano de mi colegio.
El número uno es **el patio**. El dos
es _____, el tres es _____, el
cuatro es _____, el número cinco
es _____, y el seis es _____.

Un abrazo,
Leticia

9 ✍ **Dibuja un plano de tu colegio. Escribe una carta similar.**

C ¿Qué hay en la clase?

10 ☐ **Mira y escucha.**

7 la puerta

2 las estanterías

6 la ventana

3 las sillas

5 las mesas

1 la pizarra

4 la mesa del profesor

Pronunciación

In Spanish the letter **r** is 'rolled'. When you see **rr**, the sound is even stronger!

r = puerta   estantería   laboratorio   **rr** = pizarra

11 **Escucha a Goreti y completa el cuadro.**

12 **Ahora tú. ¿Qué hay en *tu* clase? Escribe una lista.**

Aventura Semanal

Hay clases, hay biblioteca
Hay sala de vídeo
Hay clases, hay biblioteca
Hay sala de vídeo
Hay en mi colegio sí
Hay en mi colegio no
Hay en mi colegio sí
Hay en mi colegio no

Hay patio, hay laboratorio
Hay gimnasio y comedor
Hay patio, hay laboratorio
Hay gimnasio y comedor
Hay en mi colegio sí
Hay en mi colegio no
Hay en mi colegio sí
Hay en mi colegio no

La canción

¡Ya sabes!

¿Dónde **estudias**?
Estudio en el colegio...

Vocabulario del colegio: el laboratorio, la biblioteca, el gimnasio, la clase, etc.
Vocabulario de la clase: la pizarra, las estanterías, las sillas, la mesa, la ventana, etc.

¿Qué **hay** en tu colegio?   ¿Qué **hay** en tu clase?
Hay un patio.   **Hay una** pizarra.
Hay clase**s**.   **Hay** mesas.

En serio ...

Autoevaluación Tú y tu colegio

1 ¡Sabes saludar?
Escribe 4 saludos. Ejemplo ¡Hola!

(4 puntos)

2 ¡Qué tal?

(3 puntos)

3 Escribe los números 0 a 19.
Ejemplo Cero, ...

(19 puntos)

0   *6*   **7**   *9*   **11**
12   **14**   **15**   **19**

4 Escribe *tu* número de teléfono.
Ejemplo Dos nueve siete nueve nueve tres

(6 puntos)

0   *3*   **6**   **8**   *1*
7   **9**   **2**   **5**   **4**

5 Escribe 8 objetos de la cartera.
Ejemplo un lapicero

(16 puntos)

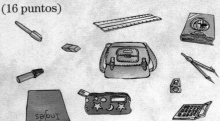

6 Escribe los días de la semana.

(7 puntos)

1	4	7
Lu	Ju	Do

7 Escribe 7 asignaturas.
Ejemplo matemáticas

(7 puntos)

 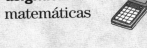

8 Escribe 6 objetos de la clase.
Ejemplo la mesa

(12 puntos)

¡no escribas aquí!

9 Escribe 6 cosas del colegio.
Ejemplo el patio

(12 puntos)

10 ¡Sabes preguntar?
Escribe las preguntas.

(14 puntos)

1 ¿.......? Ana Martínez.
2 ¿.......? M-A-R-T-Í-N-E-Z
3 ¿.......? 13 años.
4 ¿.......? Bien.
5 ¿.......? En el colegio Miraflores.
6 ¿.......? En mi colegio hay un patio, un laboratorio.
7 ¿.......? Matemáticas, francés.

A

Total = /100

... y en broma

Ahora completa tu ficha.

Mi nombre es ....

Tengo .... años.

Mi número de teléfono es ....

Mi colegio es ....

Mis asignaturas son ....

En mi colegio hay ....

En mi cartera tengo ....

¡no escribas aquí!

La canción

Estudio matemáticas, estudio inglés,
Estudio naturales, y francés.
Estudio lengua, dibujo y español,
Estudio ciencias, ¡qué follón!

Juego de la oca

Mi familia

● *Hablar de tu familia.*

A ¿Tienes hermanos?

1   Mira y escucha.

¡Hola!
Me llamo Raúl.
Éste es mi padre, Pepe.
Ésta es mi madre, Rosita.
Éste es mi hermano,
Gustavo. ¿Y tú? ¿Tienes
hermanos?

Sí. Tengo una hermana.
Y tú, Leticia, ¿tienes hermanos?

No.
No tengo hermanos.

2   Presenta tus hermanos a tus compañeros(as). Si no tienes hermanos, ¡inventa!

Ejemplo ¡Hola! Éste es mi hermano Juan; ésta es mi hermana María.

Éste es mi herman**o**.
Ésta es mi herman**a**.
Ést**e** es Pepe.
Ést**a** es Rosita.

Tengo un hermano. ☀
Tengo dos hermanos. ☀ ☀
Tengo una hermana. ☀
Tengo dos hermanas. ☀ ☀
Tengo dos hermanos
(un hermano y una hermana). ☀ ☀
No tengo hermanos. ☀ ☀

147

144

3 Une el chico/la chica con el dibujo.

a   b   c   d   e

Ahora escribe frases. **Ejemplo** Sonia: Tengo un hermano.

4 Pregunta a tus compañeros(as): ¿Cuántos hermanos tienes?

5 Une los hermanos.

¿Cómo se llama tu hermana?

Mi hermana se llama Isabel.

Leticia   Tessa

Jaime   Goreti   Carlos

Isabel   Marisa   Iñigo   María

Escucha y comprueba.

B **Mi familia** **6** Mira el árbol familiar de Raúl.

Escucha y completa las frases con los nombres.

mi padre

 mi abuela

 mi abuelo

mi madre

yo   mi hermano

Ejemplo

1 Mi padre se llama ____Pepe____.

2 Mi madre se llama _____.

3 Mi hermano se llama _____.

4 Mi abuelo se llama _____.

5 Mi abuela se llama _____.

Rosita   Pepe   Rafael

Nicolasa   Gustavo

7 Dibuja el árbol familiar de tu compañero(a). Habla con tu compañero(a).

Ejemplo Estudiante A: ¿Cómo se llama tu padre? Estudiante B: Mi padre se llama Michael.

8 ¿Qué familia es? Une los chicos con sus familias.

¡Atención!

mi hermano mayor = my big brother
mi hermano menor = my little brother

mi hermana mayor = my big sister
mi hermana menor = my little sister

Pronunciación

In Spanish, the letter '**h**' is silent. Escucha.

hermano   **hermana**   **historia**
hotel   **habla**   **Héctor**

C **9** Lee la carta de Tessa. ¿Quién es quién? Busca las nuevas palabras en el diccionario.

¡Hola Leticia!

¿Qué tal? Te mando unas fotos de mi familia. Mi padre se llama Martín y mi madre se llama Rosa María. Mi hermana se llama Isabel. Tengo dos abuelos y dos abuelas. Los padres de mi padre se llaman David y Winifred. Los padres de mi madre se llaman Rosa y Manuel. Mi tío se llama José Luis y mi tía Bárbara. Mi prima se llama Ana. Charlotte es mi prima también; es un bebé. Tengo otro primo. Se llama Raúl. ¿Y tu familia? Háblame de tu familia en tu carta.

Un abrazo,
Tessa

10 Escribe una frase para cada persona. **Ejemplo** Martín es el padre.

11 Escribe una carta a Tessa. Habla de *tu* familia.

D Los quintillizos de Huelva

12 Quintillizos: cinco niños iguales. Lee el artículo.

QUINTILLIZOS DE HUELVA CINCO DE FAMILIA ...Y CINCO MAS

Luis, Agustín, Francisco, Fermín y Juan Carlos tienen cinco años y son quintillizos. Tienen tres hermanos mayores: Pedro tiene catorce años, José tiene trece años y Fernando tiene diez años. El padre se llama José Antonio y la madre María. Ésta es una familia famosa y supernumerosa.

Los quintillizos de Huelva.

1 ¿Cuántas personas hay en total en la familia?

2 ¿Cuántos hermanos hay en total?

3 ¿Cómo se llama el hermano mayor?

4 ¿Cuántos años tienen los quintillizos?

Aventura Semanal – ¿Sabes?

In English, we often use familiar names for members of our families, e.g. Mum and Dad. Here are some Spanish ones:

madre → mamá	hermano → tato	abuela → abuelita	abuelo → abuelito
padre → papá	hermana → tata	abuela → yaya	abuelo → yayo

¡Ya sabes!

Éste es mi padre.
Ésta es mi madre.

El vocabulario de la familia: el padre, la madre, el hermano, la hermana, el abuelo, la abuela, el primo, la prima, el tío, la tía, el bebé.

¿**Tienes** hermanos?
Sí, **tengo** dos hermanos.
No, no tengo hermanos.

Tengo una hermana **mayor** y un hermano **menor**.

¿Cómo **se llama** tu padre?
Se llama Pepe.

¿De dónde eres?

O B J E T I V O

- *Decir de dónde eres y qué idiomas hablas.*
- *Hablar de nacionalidades.*

A ¿De dónde eres?

I 🔊 **Escucha.**

4 Carol
Irlanda

5 Andrew
Escocia

6 David
Gales

3 Alejandro
Estados Unidos

7 Latoya
Inglaterra

2 Javier
México

Me llamo Héctor.
Soy de Colombia.

I Héctor
Colombia

9 Celia
Cuba

8 Elena
España

¡Atención!

Colombia = Columbia
Irlanda = Ireland
Inglaterra = England
Cuba = Cuba
México = Mexico
Gales = Wales
España = Spain
Escocia = Scotland
Estados
Unidos = U.S.A.

treinta y ocho

2 Escribe el país con la nacionalidad.

Nacionalidad	País
1 mexicano/mexicana	México
2 colombiano/colombiana	
3 cubano/cubana	
4 irlandés/irlandesa	
5 escocés/escocesa	
6 inglés/inglesa	
7 galés/galesa	
8 español/española	
9 estadounidense	

¡no escribas aquí!

Me llamo Javier. Soy de México. Soy mexicano.

Escucha y comprueba.

3 Ahora tú. Habla con tus compañeros(as).
Usa *tu* nacionalidad o adopta una nacionalidad.

Ejemplo
Estudiante A: ¿De dónde eres?
Estudiante B: Soy de Cuba. Soy cubano. ¿Y tú?

SOS **Gramática** SOS

145

Javier es mexicano.
María es mexicana.
John es inglés.
Latoya es inglesa.
Raúl es español.
Elena es española.

B ¿De dónde eres?

4 Escucha y completa el cuadro.

¿De dónde eres?

Soy española y soy inglesa. Mi padre es inglés y mi madre es española.

Estefanía

Miguel

Fernando

Inés

	inglés(a)	argentino(a)	español(a)	colombiano(a)	mexicano(a)
Tessa	✓		✓		
Estefanía					
Fernando			¡no escribas aquí!		
Miguel					
Inés					

5 Tessa habla de sus amigas. Une el nombre, la nacionalidad y el país.

Marlene

Jasia

Victoria

Elena

1 Victoria	a **Bosnia**	i *inglesa*
2 Elena	b **Grecia**	j *española*
3 Carol	c **Jamaica**	k *turca*
4 Amra	d **Paquistán**	l *bosnia*
5 Jasia	e **Inglaterra**	m *jamaicana*
6 Maria	f **Turquía**	n *irlandesa*
7 Pinar	g **España**	o *griega*
8 Marlene	h **Irlanda**	p *paquistaní*

Maria

Carol

Pinar

Amra

Ahora escribe frases. Incluye a los amigos de Tessa: Okan (Turquía), Angelos (Grecia), Mehul (Paquistán).

Ejemplo Victoria es de Inglaterra. Es inglesa.

6 Adopta una nacionalidad. Pregunta a tu compañero(a): ¿De dónde eres?

Ejemplo Soy de España. Soy española.

C ¿Qué idiomas hablas?

7 Tessa pregunta a un grupo de amigos y amigas. Escucha al grupo. ¿Cuántos dicen sí? ¿Cuántos dicen no? ¿Cuántos dicen un poco?

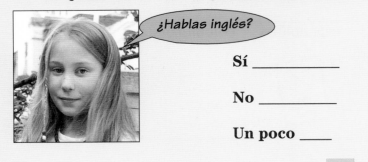
¿Hablas inglés?

Sí _____

No _____

Un poco _____

¡Atención!

alemán = German
español = Spanish
francés = French
griego = Greek
inglés = English

8 ¿Qué idiomas hablas?

Qué idiomas hablas?

Hablo inglés, español,
y un poco de alemán.
¿Y tú?

Escucha a los chicos y a las chicas y completa el cuadro.

	español	inglés	francés	alemán	griego
Tessa	✔	✔		✔	
Raúl					
Leticia					
Evi					
Elisa					

¡no escribas aquí!

9 ¿Qué idiomas hablan tus amigos(as)?

Ejemplos   ¿chino?   ¿bengalí?   ¿italiano?   ¿árabe?

Aventura Semanal – ¿Sabes?

¿Hablas español?

En español hay muchas palabras similares a otros idiomas:

Robot **radio** televisión *vídeo* automóvil

autobús taxi chocolate teléfono **piano**

¡Ya sabes!

¿De dónde **eres**?
Soy de México. **Soy** mexicano.

¿De dónde **es** Latoya?
Latoya **es** de Inglaterra.
Es inglesa.

¿Qué idiomas **hablas**?
Hablo español y francés.

Los países: España, Gales, Cuba, etc.
Las nacionalidades: inglés/inglesa,
mexicano/mexicana, griego/griega, etc.
Los idiomas: español, alemán, inglés, etc.

8

Vivo en Madrid

OBJETIVO

● *Decir dónde vives.*   ● *Hablar de los colores.*

A Mi ciudad

1 🔊 Escucha.

¿Dónde vives?

Vivo en Londres, en Inglaterra. ¿Y tú?

Vivo en Madrid, en España.

2 🔊 ¿Dónde viven? Escucha y une los chicos y las chicas con las ciudades. Ejemplo 1 = e

1 Álvaro

2 Ana

3 Héctor

4 Verónica

5 Javier

a Barcelona
España

b Bogotá
Colombia

c Ciudad de México
México

d Nueva York
Estados Unidos

e Madrid
España

3 💬 ¿Y tú? Adopta una personalidad. Pregunta a tus compañeros(as).

Ejemplo Estudiante A: Me llamo Ana. Vivo en Barcelona. ¿Y tú? ¿Dónde vives?
          Estudiante B: Vivo en ...
          Cambia.

B Más números

4 Escucha estos números.

20 21 22 23 30 34 35 36 40

47 48 49 50 60 70 80 90 100

Indica estos números:

veintitrés

cuarenta y siete

treinta y cuatro

cuarenta y nueve   sesenta   cien

cincuenta   noventa

C ¿Dónde vives?

Estudia. Éstos son ejemplos de nombres típicos de calles en España.

Calle del Monasterio de Rueda   Avenida de las Fuentes
Plaza de España   Paseo de la Constitución

Calle

Avenida

Plaza

Paseo

Escucha.

5 ¿Dónde viven Jaime, Leticia, Elena y Raúl? Indica las calles.

SOS Gramática SOS

El verbo: **vivir**

(yo) **vivo** en Londres.
(tú) **vives** en Madrid.
(él/ella) **vive** en París.

 152

Escucha otra vez. Indica los números.

Ejemplo Jaime vive en el número 86.

6 Pregunta a tus compañeros(as): ¿Dónde vives?

Ejemplo Vivo en la calle _____, número_____.

Escribe la información en la agenda.

Nombre ....
Dirección ....
....
¡no escribas aquí!
....
Teléfono ....

D Los colores

7 Mira los colores. Escucha y repite.

1 naranja
2 rosa
3 rojo
4 blanco
5 amarillo
6 verde
7 gris
8 azul
9 marrón
10 negro

SOS Gramática SOS

Masculino
un estuche rojo
             amarillo
un estuche verde
             azul
             marrón

Femenino
una cartera roja
             amarilla
una cartera verde
             azul
             marrón

145

8 Escucha y pinta los números.

45 13 70 25 63 89

9 ¿De qué color es la bandera de España? Escribe los colores de las banderas.

España	Colombia	México
rojo	_____	_____
amarillo	_____	_____
_____		

10 💬 **Más banderas. Dicta y pinta los colores con tu compañero(a).**

Estudiante A: ¿De qué color es la bandera de España?

Estudiante B: Rojo, amarillo y rojo.

España

Chile

Venezuela

11 📖 **Hay más de 300 millones de personas que hablan español en 23 países. Mira el mapa en las páginas 10 – 11. ¿Qué países son?**

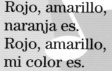

Aventura Semanal

Canción de los colores

Rojo, amarillo,	Azul y rosa,
naranja es.	amarillo, limón,
Rojo, amarillo,	negro, rojo,
mi color es.	gris y marrón.

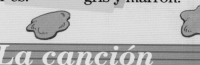

La canción

¡Ya sabes!

¿Dónde **vives**?
Vivo en en Bogotá, en Colombia.

¿Dónde **vive** Luis?
Luis **vive** en la calle Asalto.

Los colores: naranja, rojo, blanco, verde, gris, azul, marrón, rosa, negro, amarillo.
Un estuch**e** roj**o**; una carter**a** roj**a**.
Los números: 20, 21, 30, 40, ... 90, 100.
Vocabulario de la ciudad: la calle, el paseo, la avenida, la plaza, etc.

9

¿Cómo es?

O B J E T I V O

● *Describir a personas y animales.*

A ¿Tienes animales en casa?

1 ¿Qué animales tienes en casa? Escucha y repite.

1 un gato

2 un perro

3 un pájaro

4 un conejo

5 un ratón

6 un pez

7 un caballo

8 una tortuga

Une el animal con el nombre. Ejemplo 1 = c

Escucha y comprueba.

2 Escucha a los chicos y chicas. ¿Tienen animales en casa?

	Leticia	Elena	Tessa	Goreti	Héctor	Carlos
perro	1		¡no escribas aquí!			
gato						
pájaro						
tortuga						

3 ¿Y tú? ¿Tienes animales en casa? Habla con tu compañero(a). Si no tienes animales en casa, ¡inventa!   **Ejemplo** Sí. Tengo dos gatos. ¿Y tú?

B   ¿Cómo es?

Tengo un perro, un caballo, un ratón y un gato. Mi perro es feo. Mi caballo es grande. Mi ratón es pequeño. Mi gato es bonito.

4 Escucha a Leticia, a Tessa y a Héctor. Describen a sus animales. Completa las fichas de los animales.

Leticia

Tessa

Héctor

Ficha
animal _____
nombre *Patras*
años _____
color _____
descripción _____

Ficha
animal _____
nombre *Zipi*
años _____
color _____
descripción _____

Ficha
animal _____
nombre *Pío*
años _____
color _____
descripción _____

5 Lee la carta de Elena y escribe las fichas de sus animales.

¡Hola!

Me llamo Elena. Vivo en Zaragoza. Tengo doce años. Tengo dos tortugas en casa. Una se llama Chispa. Es pequeña; es de color verde y marrón y tiene tres años. La otra tortuga se llama Concha. Es grande y tiene cinco años. Es también verde y marrón.

Un abrazo,
Elena

6 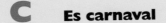 **Habla con tu compañero(a) y completa la ficha de su animal.**

Prepara una ficha de *tu* animal.

Pronunciación

The ñ in Spanish sounds like ca**ny**on in English. Escucha.

ñ = peque**ñ**o, a**ñ**o, compa**ñ**ero, ni**ñ**o

C   Es carnaval

7 **Tessa dibuja disfraces de carnaval.**

bajo

rubio

feo

gordo

a el monstruo

alta

guapa

morena

delgada

b la princesa

¡Atención!

el disfraz = fancy dress costume (singular)
los disfraces = fancy dress costumes (plural)

Gramática
SOS SOS

Masculino
-o peque**ño**
-o gord**o**
-e grand**e**

Femenino
-a peque**ña**
-a gord**a**
-e grand**e**

145

 Escucha.

8 **Describe al monstruo, a la bruja, al esqueleto y a la princesa.**
Usa las palabras de Actividad 7. Ejemplo El monstruo es bajo y feo.

a el monstruo   **b** la bruja   **c** el esqueleto   **d** la princesa

D Mi familia y mis amigos

9 Elena describe a sus padres, a su hermano, y a su amiga Tessa. Lee la carta y completa con estas palabras:

rubio/rubia   alto/alta   guapo/guapa   delgado/delgada   moreno/morena

¡Hola!

Te mando una foto de mi familia y mi amiga Tessa. Mi madre se llama Gloria. Es _____, _____ y _____. Mi padre se llama José Luis. Es _____ y _____ y tiene gafas y bigote. Mi hermano también se llama José Luis pero le llamamos Pepe. Es también _____ y _____ y tiene gafas. Es muy _____. Tessa es mi amiga. Vive en Inglaterra. Es _____ y tiene once años. Yo soy _____, _____ y _____. ¿Y tú y tu familia?

Un abrazo,
Elena

Escucha y comprueba.

10 Escribe una carta a Elena. Describe a tu familia y a un(a) amigo(a).

11 ¿Tienes fotos de tu familia, de tus amigos(as) y de tus animales? Habla con tus compañeros(as).

Aventura Semanal – ¿Sabes?

El carnaval es muy popular en España y en Latinoamérica. Se celebra en febrero. Hay fiestas, bailes de disfraces y competiciones de disfraces. Hay desfiles por las calles. El carnaval más famoso en España es el carnaval de Tenerife en las islas Canarias.

¡Ya sabes!

¿**Tienes** animales en casa?
Sí, **tengo** dos perros.

¿**Cómo es** tu gato? **Es** grande y bonito.
¿**Cómo es** tu herman**o**? Es moren**o**, alt**o** y guap**o**.
¿**Cómo es** tu amig**a**? Es pequeñ**a**, rubi**a** y delgad**a**.

Los animales: un gato, una tortuga, un caballo, un ratón, un pez, etc.

Vocabulario del carnaval:
disfraces, desfiles, el monstruo, la princesa, el esqueleto, etc.

LECCIÓN 10

Mi cumpleaños

● *Decir cuándo es tu cumpleaños.* ● *Decir la fecha.*

A El calendario

1 Mira y escucha.

1	**enero**	4	**abril**	7	**julio**	10	**octubre**	
2	**febrero**	5	**mayo**	8	**agosto**	11	**noviembre**	
3	**marzo**	6	**junio**	9	**septiembre**	12	**diciembre**	

2 Habla con tu compañero(a). Estudiante A: Dice un número del uno al doce.
Estudiante B: Responde con el mes.

Cinco.

Mayo.

¡Atención!

2 - 10 - 1956
el día - el mes - el año

hoy = today
la fecha = the date

Continúa.

3 Escribe el mes.
Ejemplo 1 - 3 = marzo

1	2 - 10	**6**	1 - 1	
2	6 - 4	**7**	29 - 2	
3	3 - 11	**8**	6 - 6	
4	15 - 7	**9**	19 - 8	
5	25 - 12	**10**	13 - 5	

 ¿Qué mes falta? Escucha y comprueba.

4 **Escucha la fecha y escribe los números.**

Ejemplo

...el veintiuno de septiembre.

5 **Dicta cinco fechas a tu compañero(a). Tu compañero(a) escribe las fechas. Ahora cambia.**

6 **¿Qué día es hoy? Escribe la fecha en palabras.**

Ejemplo

¿Qué día es hoy?

Hoy es el quince de febrero.

1 15 - 2 = El quince de febrero.
2 17 - 8 =
3 21 - 10 =
4 13 - 3 =
5 7 - 12 =
6 30 - 7 =

7 **¡Canta la canción!**

Uno de enero, dos de febrero, tres de marzo, cuatro de abril.

Cinco de mayo, seis de junio, siete de julio, San Fermín.

B ¿Cuándo es tu cumpleaños?

8 **Mira y escucha.**

Mi cumpleaños es el trece de septiembre.

¿Cuándo es tu cumpleaños?

Ahora une la fecha con el chico/la chica.

   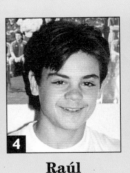 

1	2	3	4	5
Tessa	**Jaime**	**Isabel**	**Raúl**	**Goreti**
a 24 - 4	b 5 - 8	c 17 - 6	d 27 - 11	e 14 - 5

9  **Pregunta a tus compañeros(as) y completa la agenda.**

Los cumpleaños de mis compañeros(as)

Nombre .... *Fecha de cumpleaños*

¡no escribas aquí!

Escribe en tu cuaderno o en el ordenador la base de datos de la clase. ¿Qué mes es más popular?

C La postal de cumpleaños

10  **¡Canta la canción de cumpleaños!**

Cumpleaños feliz
Cumpleaños feliz
Te deseamos todos
Cumpleaños feliz

11 **Mira las postales.**

12 **Dibuja una postal de cumpleaños. Escribe a un(a) amigo(a).**

Aventura Semanal – ¿Sabes?

¡martes día trece = Friday 13th!

Martes y trece. En España y en Latinoamérica el martes día trece significa mala suerte (bad luck). El equivalente en Inglaterra es viernes y trece.

LOS MARTES Y 13 HASTA
EL AÑO 2.000
*1994: En septiembre y en diciembre.
*1995: En junio.
*1996: En febrero y en agosto.
*1997: En mayo.
*1998: En enero y en octubre.
*1999: En abril y en julio.
*2000: En junio.

¡Ya sabes!

¿Qué día es hoy?
Hoy es el veinticinco de enero.

¿Cuándo es tu cumpleaños?
Mi cumpleaños es el treinta de junio.
Feliz cumpleaños.

Los meses: enero, febrero, marzo, abril, mayo, junio, julio, agosto, septiembre, octubre, noviembre, diciembre.

Las fechas: el uno de enero, el dos de febrero, el tres de marzo, etc.

En serio …

Autoevaluación Tú y los demás

1 **Tú eres Bea. Mira tu árbol familiar y escribe 10 frases.**
Ejemplo Mi hermano se llama Javier.
(20 puntos)

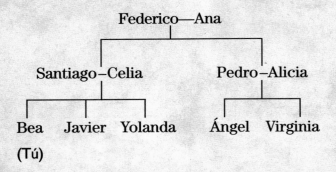

Federico—Ana

Santiago–Celia   Pedro–Alicia

Bea   Javier   Yolanda   Ángel   Virginia

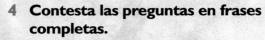
(Tú)

2 **Escribe las preguntas a Bea.**
Ejemplo ¿Cómo te llamas? Me llamo Bea.
(6 puntos)

1 ¿...?   Tengo dos hermanos.
2 ¿...?   Santiago y Celia.
3 ¿...?   Sí, tengo un abuelo y una abuela.

3 **Escribe los nombres de 7 países y nacionalidades.**
(14 puntos)

¡no escribas aquí!

4 **Contesta las preguntas en frases completas.**
(14 puntos)

1 ¿De dónde eres?
2 ¿De dónde es tu amigo(a)?
3 ¿Qué idiomas hablas?
4 ¿Dónde vives?
5 ¿Cuál es tu número de teléfono?
6 ¿Dónde vive tu amigo(a)?
7 ¿Dónde viven tus abuelos?

5 **¿Qué colores hay?**
Ejemplo verde
(5 puntos)

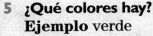

6 **Escribe los números en palabras.**
Ejemplo 98 = noventa y ocho
(14 puntos)

20 29 **50** **67**
35 47 78

7 **Escribe 5 animales y cómo son.**
Ejemplo El pájaro es pequeño.
(10 puntos)

8 **Completa el calendario.**
(7 puntos)

FEBRERO	ABRIL		

		JULIO	

SEPTIEMBRE			DICIEMBRE

9 **Escribe las fechas.**
Ejemplo 8-9 = el ocho de septiembre
(10 puntos)

10-5 **3-3** 7-11 **30-8** 27-6

B

Total =   /100

... y en broma

Lee las cartas de los(las) amigos(as).

Hola, soy una chica alemana de 18 años y estudio español. No hablo mucho español pero escribo un poco. Hablo también inglés y francés. ¡Busco amigos y amigas internacionales!

Escribe a: **Maria Schorn, PO Box 54, Neustadt Strasse, Frankfurt, Alemania.**

Hola amigo, ¿Eres inglés o de Estados Unidos? ¿Tienes de 11 a 15 años? Escribe en inglés o en español a Marta. Tengo 12 años y mi dirección es:

Calle Montserrat, 222, Valencia, España.

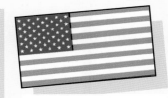

¡Hola! Me llamo **Carmen Rodríguez Ruíz.** Tengo catorce años. Soy alta y morena. Soy mexicana. Mi color favorito es el azul y tengo un gato bonito. ¿Tienes animales? Escribe a **Avenida Lucio Blanco, 98, México DF CP02400.**

Hola, soy un chico moreno, delgado, alto y guapo. Tengo 15 años y soy de Barcelona. ¿Tienes de 12 a 17 años? Escribe a **Luis, Avenida Gracia, número 18, 495008, Barcelona, España.**

¿Quién es?

1 Mi amigo(a) tiene dieciocho años.
2 Mi amiga es alta y morena.
3 Mi amigo(a) habla cuatro idiomas.
4 Vivo en los Estados Unidos. ¿Quién es mi amigo(a)?
5 Mi amigo(a) tiene un gato.
6 Mi amigo(a) vive en Alemania.
7 Mi amigo(a) habla español pero no es de España.
8 Tengo once años. Mi amigo(a) es ...

¡Ahora escribe *tu* anuncio!

¿Qué hora es?

● *Decir qué hora es.*   ● *Decir qué haces en tu tiempo libre.*

A ¿Qué hora es?

1   Mira los dibujos y escucha.

a

b

c

d

e

1 ● ¿Qué hora es? ■ Son las diez. ● ¡Oh no! ¡Tengo matemáticas!	**2** ● Niño, son las siete. ■ ¡Oh no!
3 ● ¿Qué hora es? ■ S-s-son las doce.	**4** ● ¿Qué hora es? ■ Son las once. ● ¡Mi tren!

5 ● ¿Qué hora es?
■ Son las nueve.
● ¡Las nueve!

2   Ahora une los diálogos con los dibujos. Ejemplo a = 2

Escucha y comprueba.

> **¡Atención!**
>
> **el reloj** = a clock or a watch
> **cada** = each or every

3   En esta casa los relojes no funcionan. ¿Qué hora es en cada reloj? Escribe frases.

Escucha y comprueba.

4 **Habla con tu compañero(a).**

Estudiante A: Dice la hora.

 *Son las once.*

Estudiante B: Completa el reloj.

Ahora cambia.

¿Qué hora es?
Es la una.
(singular)

¿Qué hora es?
Son las dos.
(plural)

148

B ¿A qué hora tienes matemáticas?

5 **Escucha a Tessa y a Elena. Escribe la hora.**

¿A qué hora tienes matemáticas?

A las nueve.

	Tessa	Elena
ciencias naturales	___	___
matemáticas	9.00	___
inglés	___	___
gimnasia	___	___
dibujo	___	___
lengua	___	___

¡no escribas aquí!

6 **Habla con tu compañero(a).**

Ejemplo Estudiante A: ¿A qué hora tienes gimnasia?
Estudiante B: Tengo gimnasia a las diez.

Continúa.

¡Atención!

recreo = playtime/break
de... a ... = from ... to ...
de la mañana = in the morning
de la tarde = in the afternoon

7 **Escucha a Goreti y a Sara. Completa el cuadro con G = Goreti, S = Sara.**

La hora	Las asignaturas						
	matemáticas	español	dibujo	ciencias naturales	francés	gimnasia	inglés
9-10	G						
10-11							
11-12							

¡no escribas aquí!

8 **Habla con tu compañero(a). Estudiante A: Adopta el horario de Goreti.**
Estudiante B: Adopta el horario de Sara.

Ahora habla de *tu* horario.

Ejemplo Estudiante A: El lunes de las nueve a las diez tengo inglés. ¿Y tú?
Estudiante B: El martes de las diez a las once tengo ...

C ¿Qué días vas al club?

9   Estudia.

¿A qué hora vas al club, Héctor?

Voy al club a las seis.

¿Y Elena? ¿A qué hora va al club?

Elena va al club a las cinco.

SOS Gramática SOS

El verbo: **ir**

(yo) **voy** al club
(tú) **vas** al club
(él/ella) **va** al club

153

10   Escucha a Sara, a Héctor y a Goreti. ¿Qué días van al club? ¿Cuántos días van al club? ¿A qué hora van al club?

11   ¿Y tú? Lee los anuncios. Imagina que vas a un club. Habla con tu compañero(a).

Musaraña
Horario del
Club Musaraña

LUNES Y MIÉRCOLES:
5:00 a 7:30 h. de la tarde.

MARTES Y VIERNES:
10:30 a 1:30 h. de la mañana y
4:00 a 6:30 h. de la tarde.

Horario del
Club A DALLA
MARTES Y VIERNES:
6:00 a 8:00 h. de la tarde.
MIÉRCOLES Y JUEVES:
10:00 a 12:00 h. de la mañana y
3:30 a 5:30 h. de la tarde.

CENTRO CULTURAL DELICIAS
Horario del
Centro Cultural Delicias
MARTES Y JUEVES:
5:30 a 7:00 h. de la tarde.
LUNES Y VIERNES:
10:00 a 12:30 h. de la mañana y
3:30 a 6:00 h. de la tarde.

D Las cinco y media

Mira y escucha.

¿Qué hora es?

Son las cinco y media.

12   Pregunta a tu compañero(a):
¿Qué hora es?

Escucha y comprueba.

13 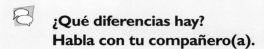 **Escucha el programa de radio e indica las fechas de los conciertos de Mecano.**

	Sevilla	Madrid	Barcelona	Bilbao
El mes		febrero		
El día			¡no escribas aquí!	
La hora				

En el programa hay errores. Lee el auténtico calendario de Mecano.

Conciertos de Mecano

En Sevilla, el lunes 30 de enero a las 5.30 de la tarde. En Madrid actúa Mecano el día 11 de febrero, sábado, a las 7.30, y en Barcelona concierto de Mecano el viernes, 24 de febrero, a las 10.30 de la noche. El concierto de Bilbao es el jueves, día 2 de marzo, en el teatro Principal.

¿Qué diferencias hay?
Habla con tu compañero(a).

Ejemplo En Sevilla el concierto es en enero **no** en febrero; es el lunes **no el** martes...

14 **Ahora prepara un programa de radio con tus compañeros(as).**

Escribe un calendario de conciertos de *tu* grupo favorito.

Aventura Semanal

¿Qué hora es?

Buenos días, buenos días
¿Qué hora es? ¿Qué hora es?
Son las ocho, son las nueve
son las diez, son las diez.
Llego tarde, llego tarde
otra vez, otra vez.
Buenos días, buenos días
¿Qué hora es? ¿Qué hora es?

La canción

¡Ya sabes!

La hora: ¿Qué hora **es**? **Es** la una.
Son las nueve. **Son** las nueve y media.

¿A qué hora tienes gimnasia?
De nueve **a** diez.

¿Cuántos días tienes español? Dos días.

¿Qué días **vas** al club?
Voy al club el viernes y el sábado.
¿A qué hora **va** Elena al club?
Va a las cinco.

12

En el club

A Éste es mi club

I 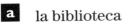 **Escucha a Joaquín. Habla de su club. Mira los dibujos.**

a la biblioteca

b la piscina

c la cafetería

d la sala
de juegos

f la sala
de vídeo

g la mesa
de ping-pong

e el taller
de arte

h el taller
de manualidades

 Lee y une los dibujos con las frases. Escucha y comprueba.

¿Masculino o femenino?	¿Singular o plural?
SOS Gramática SOS	
Éste es **el** club.	masculino, singular
Ést**os son** unos chic**os** del club.	masculino, plural
Ést**a** es **la** biblioteca.	femenino, singular
Ést**as son** las mes**as** de ping-pong.	femenino, plural

147

2 ✏️ **Mira el plano y completa:**

Ejemplo **I** = **Ésta es** la biblioteca.

2 ___ ___ la cafetería.
3 ___ ___ el taller de arte.
4 ___ ___ la mesa de ping-pong.
5 ___ ___ la piscina.

3 📼 **Escucha. Daniel, Elena y Héctor describen su club. Completa el cuadro.**

Daniel			
Héctor			
Elena			

 Daniel

 Héctor

 Elena

4 💬 **¿Qué hay en tu club? Habla con tus compañeros(a). Si no tienes un club: Estudiante A adopta el club de Daniel. Estudiante B adopta el club de Elena. Estudiante C adopta el club de Héctor.**

Ejemplo En mi club hay un taller de arte.

B ¿Cómo es el club?

5 📖 **Lee la carta de Tessa.**

💬 **Contesta las preguntas:**

1 ¿Cómo se llama el club?
2 ¿Cómo es el club? ¿Qué hay?
3 ¿Cómo se llama la mejor amiga de Tessa?
4 ¿Cómo es la chica?
5 ¿Cuándo va Tessa al club?
6 ¿Adónde va en el verano?

✏️ **Contesta la carta de Tessa. Describe *tu* club.**

Querida Elena:
Éste es mi club. Se llama Centro Cultural Delicias. Es un club estupendo y hay muchos chicos y chicas. Hay una biblioteca. También hay una sala de juegos. Hay un taller de manualidades y una sala de vídeo.
Voy al club los lunes y los miércoles de cinco a siete de la tarde. En verano voy a un campamento con el club. Mi mejor amiga se llama Marta. Es muy simpática. El campamento de verano es muy divertido. ¿Vas a un centro cultural? ¿Cómo es? ¿Cuándo vas? ¿Vas a un campamento en el verano?
Un abrazo,
Tessa

¡Atención!

simpático(a) = nice
el campamento = summer camp
mejor amigo(a) = best friend
es divertido(a) = it's fun

6 **Lee la información sobre las actividades del club.**

ACTIVIDADES

PROYECTOS DE VÍDEO: Todos los días a las 19 h.
PROYECCIONES DE CINE: Sábados alternos 6.30h.
SESIONES DE DIBUJO Y PINTURA: 2a. semana de cada mes
EXPOSICIÓN DE FOTOGRAFÍA: Diciembre
CINE INFANTIL: Sábados alternos 6.30h.
EXCURSIONES
PROGRAMA DE RADIO: En colaboración con Radio Mai
INTERCAMBIOS con Casas de Juventud del extranjero
SALÓN DE ESTAR Y JUEGOS DE MESA
PING–PONG, MÚSICA, DEPORTES, INFORMACIÓN SOBRE
INTERCAMBIOS, VIAJES, SUBVENCIONES, VACACIONES
Y TODO TIPO DE ACTIVIDADES JUVENILES.

¿Qué actividades hay? ¿Cuándo?

¿Cómo **es el** club?
Es estupend**o**. **Es** bonit**o**. **Es** grande.

¿Cómo **es la** sala de vídeo?
Es estupend**a**. **Es** bonit**a**. **Es** grande.

¿Cómo **es el** director?
Es simpátic**o**. Joaquín **es** simpátic**o**.

¿Cómo **es la** chica.
Es simpátic**a**.

a + el → al
Voy **al** club.

de + el → del
El director **del** club.

7 **Prepara un póster para tu club ideal. ¿Qué actividades hay? ¿Cuándo? ¿Cómo es?**

C ¿Qué juegos hay?

8 **Escucha y mira los juegos.**

Une el juego con el nombre. Ejemplo 1 = e

1 el futbolín
2 el parchís
3 la vídeo consola
4 la oca
5 el Monopoly
6 el Scrabble
7 las cartas
8 la lotería

9 🗨 **Elige cinco de los juegos de Actividad 8 y habla con tus compañeros(as).**

Ejemplo

¿A qué juegas?

Juego a la vídeo consola.

Juego al futbolín.

10 🗨 **Encuesta. ¿Qué juegos son más populares en *tu* clase?**

Aventura Semanal – ¿Sabes?

Anuncios de juguetes

Mira el anuncio de juguetes populares.
¿Hay estos juguetes en las tiendas de tu país?

Juegos

Juegos de mesa, juegos de acción, juegos de destreza, juegos de lógica, juegos pedagógicos, juegos para niños, juegos para todas las edades. ¡Y muchos más!

¡Ya sabes!

Éste es mi club.
Ésta es mi amiga.
Éstos son mis amigos.
Éstas son mis amigas.

¿Cómo es?
El director **es** simpático.
Mi amiga **es** simpática.

(yo) **juego a la** oca.
¿A qué **juegas**?
(él/ella) **juega al** futbolín.

Hay una biblioteca. **Es** grande.
No hay piscina.

Vocabulario del club: la piscina, el taller de manualidades, la sala de juegos, etc.
Los juegos: el futbolín, el ping-pong, el parchís, la vídeo consola, la oca, etc.

LECCIÓN **13**

Un helado, por favor

O B J E T I V O

● **Pedir comida y bebida.**　　● **Preguntar cuánto es.**

A Un helado, por favor

I **Mira los dibujos. Escucha y repite.**

una coca cola

un café

un helado

un té

una hamburguesa

un chocolate

un agua mineral

una pizza

un sandwich

un refresco

una galleta

un pastel

un zumo de naranja

un bocadillo

patatas fritas

queso

 Lee y comprueba.

2 **Escribe una lista de comida y una lista de bebida.**

Comida	Bebida
una hamburguesa	un chocolate

¡Atención!

la comida = food
la bebida = drink
por favor = please
gracias = thank you
toma = take (here you are)

3 **Escucha a los chicos y chicas. Indica qué comen y beben.**

| 1 | | | | | |

4 **¿Qué dicen? Escribe las frases.**

Un helado, por favor.

Comprueba con tu compañero(a).

5 **Elige 3 bebidas y 3 comidas y pide a tu compañero(a).**

Ejemplo
Estudiante A: Un zumo de naranja, por favor.
Estudiante B: Sí, toma.
Estudiante A: Gracias.

Cambia.

MENÚ

Bebida

Comida

zumo de naranja

agua mineral

refresco

chocolate

patatas fritas

hamburguesa

pizza

bocadillos

B ¿Cuánto es?

6   **Mira, escucha y repite los números.**

100   200   300   400   500

600   700   800   900   1000

7 Une los números con las palabras.

seiscientos	500
cien	300
novecientos	100
setecientos	400
trescientos	800
cuatrocientos	200
doscientos	600
quinientos	1000
ochocientos	700
mil	900

SOS Gramática SOS

Los números desde 200 cambian.

| **Masculino** | **Femenino** |
| Doscient**os** dólares. | Doscient**as** pesetas. |

¡Nota! Cien y **mil** no cambian.

| Cien dólares. | Cien pesetas. |
| Mil dólares. | Mil pesetas. |

➡ **148**

....
¡Atención!
....

dólares = $ = U.S. dollars
libras esterlinas = £ = British pounds
pesetas = ptas = Spanish pesetas

....

8 ✎ **Escribe en palabras. Ejemplo** $200 = doscientos dólares

$200   £100   800ptas   500ptas $500   1000ptas

£1000   400ptas   100ptas $300

C ¿Qué quieres?

9  **Escucha y estudia.**

¡Atención!

un yogur = a yoghurt
una gaseosa = lemonade

un zumo de naranja
un refresco
un pastel
un yogur
un helado
una gaseosa
un agua mineral

¿Qué quieres?

Quiero un pastel.

💬 **Mira el frigo e inventa un diálogo con tu compañero(a).**

10   **Escribe una lista de bebida y comida con tu compañero(a) para una fiesta de cumpleaños.**

   Escucha la lista de Tessa. Compara con tu lista. ¿Coinciden?

D ¿Cuánto es?

11   **Tessa va al supermercado y compra comida y bebida para el cumpleaños de Isabel. ¿Qué compra?**

   Mira los dibujos e indica qué compra. ¿Cuánto es cada producto? Escucha otra vez e indica el precio.

Aventura Semanal – ¿Sabes?

El dinero en España

Monedas   **Billetes**

¡Ya sabes!

¿Qué **quieres**?   **¿Cuánto es**?
Quiero un helado, por favor.   Cien pesetas.
                               Doscientas pesetas.

Los números: 100, 200, 300, ... , 800, 900, 1000.
La bebida: un zumo de naranja, un chocolate, un agua mineral, un refresco, etc.
La comida: una hamburguesa, una pizza, un pastel, un helado, las patatas fritas, etc.

Gustos y disgustos

OBJETIVO

● *Decir qué comida y bebida te gusta.*

● *Decir qué animales te gustan.*

A Me gusta el chocolate

1 Escucha las frases. Une las frases con los dibujos. **Ejemplo** $2 = c$

a Me gusta la leche.

b No me gusta la tortilla.

c Me gusta el chocolate.

d No me gustan las hamburguesas.

e Me gusta el queso

f Me gustan los plátanos.

Escucha otra vez y comprueba.

2 Estudia.

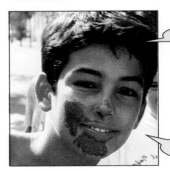

¿Te gusta la tortilla?

No, no me gusta la tortilla. ¿Te gusta el chocolate?

Sí. Me gusta el chocolate.

3 **Escucha las entrevistas y completa el cuadro.**

Las preguntas: ¿Qué comida te gusta?

¿Qué comida no te gusta?

¿Qué bebida te gusta?

¿Qué bebida no te gusta?

Indica ✔ **= Sí.**

✗ **= No.**

Tessa

Pedro

Elena

Tessa					¡no escribas aquí!				
Elena									
Pedro									

4 **Habla con tu compañero(a).**

Ejemplo

Estudiante A: ¿Te gusta el chocolate?

Estudiante B: Sí me gusta. ¿Te gusta el café?

Estudiante A: No. No me gusta.

Continúa.

SOS Gramática SOS El verbo: **gustar** ➡ 155

Me gusta	el chocolate.	(singular)
No me gusta	la tortilla.	(singular)
Me gustan	las patatas.	(plural)
No me gustan	los plátanos.	(plural)

5 **Escucha y repite.**

las salchichas

las ensaladas

las patatas

las verduras

los plátanos

las naranjas

los espaguetis

las frutas

 Ahora tú. Habla con tu compañero(a).

Ejemplo Estudiante A: ¿Te gusta(n) ...? Estudiante B: No. No me gusta(n). ¿Te gusta(n) ...?

Continúa.

6   Escucha a Tessa en McDonald's. ¿Qué quiere? Indica en el menú.

Cuarto de Libra™ con queso   McPollo™   Filete de Pescado™   McNuggets™   Happy Meal™

Descubre todo el sabor que te rodea en McDonald's™

Patatas Fritas

Ensaladas

Refrescos

Batidos

McDonald's   Sabemos lo que te gusta   Big Mac™

Sundaes™   Pastel de Manzana

7   Pregunta a tu compañero(a): ¿Qué quieres del menú? **Ejemplo** Quiero un refresco.

8   Encuesta de la clase. ¿Qué comida es más popular? ¿Qué bebida es menos popular?

B   Mis gustos

9   Lee la carta de Raúl sobre sus gustos.

Querido Jaime:

Me gusta la coca cola y me gustan las ensaladas. No me gusta el queso y no me gustan las salchichas ni las hamburguesas. Soy vegetariano porque me gustan mucho los animales. Tengo un gato muy bonito que se llama Felino. Es negro y pequeño. Le gustan mucho las hamburguesas. También le gusta la leche. ¡Pero no le gustan las ensaladas! ¿Te gustan los animales? ¿Y qué te gusta comer y beber?

Un abrazo,
Raúl

¿Qué le gusta a Raúl? Indica.

¡Atención!

o = or
no ... ni ... = neither ... nor ...
para comer = to eat
para beber = to drink
porque = because
sobre todo = especially
muy = very
vegetariano(a) = vegetarian

10   Escribe una carta similar.

11 **Completa el crucigrama.**

MONO

PÁJARO

DELFÍN

GATO

TIGRE

CONEJO

PERRO

CABALLO

Repite el trabalenguas: Tres tristes tigres comen trigo en un trigal.

12 **Escucha las entrevistas. ¿Qué animales les gustan a los chicos y chicas?**

13 **Encuesta de animales. Pregunta a tus compañeros(as): ¿Cuántos animales tienen? ¿Qué animales? ¿Cuántos perros, gatos, tortugas, etc.? ¿Cuál es el animal más popular en la clase?**

Aventura Semanal

A mi tortuga le gusta la lechuga,
a mi pez el agua mineral.

A mi perro le gusta la hamburguesa,
y un filete para cenar.

A mi ratón le gusta el queso,
a mi gato le gusta mi ratón.

A mi conejo le gusta el chocolate,
y a mi pájaro le gusta el turrón.

La canción

¡Ya sabes!

Me gusta el chocolate.
No me gusta la tortilla.

Me gustan las patatas.
No me gustan los plátanos.

¿Te gusta el chocolate?
¿Te gustan las hamburguesas?

La comida y bebida: la leche, los zumos de frutas, las salchichas, etc.

Las verduras y frutas: las patatas, las ensaladas, el plátano, la naranja, etc.

Los animales: el mono, el tigre, el delfín, etc.

LECCIÓN 15

Tú, todos los días

O B J E T I V O

- **Decir qué comes y a qué hora comes.**
- **Hablar de la vida diaria.**

A ¿Qué comes?

1 Mira los dibujos y escucha.

El desayuno   La comida   La cena

2 Escucha.

¿Qué desayunas?

Desayuno leche y cereales.

¡Atención!

desayunar = to have breakfast
comer = to eat/have lunch
cenar = to have supper/dinner

El verbo: **desayunar**	El verbo: **comer**	El verbo: **cenar**
(yo) desayuno	como	ceno
(tú) desayunas	comes	cenas
(él/ella) desayuna	come	cena

152

3 Escucha e indica qué desayunan. **1 = Leticia. 2 = Goreti. 3 = Sara. 4 = Cristian.**

la leche 4	las magdalenas	las tostadas	los cereales	el Cola Cao	las galletas

4 Pregunta a tus compañeros(as): ¿Qué desayunas?

5 Escucha y mira los dibujos.   Pregunta a tus compañeros(as).

¿Qué comes?
Como salchichas y patatas fritas.

¿Qué cenas?
Ceno ensalada y tortilla.

6 Lee la carta de Jaime.

Querida Tessa:
¿Qué tal? En tu carta me preguntas qué como y a qué hora. Pues desayuno a las ocho y media, leche y galletas. Como a las dos en el comedor del colegio. Tengo dos horas para comer. Me gustan los espaguetis, el pollo, la pizza y la ensalada. Ceno en casa con mis padres y mi hermana. Ceno a las ocho una tortilla o un bocadillo de queso.

Un abrazo,
Jaime

Completa las frases:

1 Jaime desayuna *leche y* a las _____ .

2 Jaime come _____ a las _____ .

3 Jaime cena _____ a las _____ .

B ¿Qué haces en el campamento?

7 Tessa y su amiga van al campamento este año. Tessa explica qué hace en el campamento. Une las fotos con las frases.

Ejemplo 1 = g

a Bailo.

b Toco la guitarra y canto.

c Pinto camisetas.

d Duermo la siesta.

e Escribo cartas.

f Como a las dos.

g Desayuno leche y pan.

h Hablo con mis amigos.

i Escucho música.

Escucha a Tessa y comprueba.

8 **Pregunta a tu compañero(a) y completa el cuadro.**

Sí						
No						

¡no escribas aquí!

9 **Ahora escribe frases.** **Ejemplo** Yo toco la guitarra. David canta.

C Un cantante famoso

10 Lee el artículo sobre el cantante Miguel de Ray.

Ordena las fotos con el texto.

Ejemplo 1 = d

Miguel de Ray, el famoso cantante, tiene 20 años y vive una vida normal. Éste es un día típico de Miguel:

1 10.30h. Cada día a las diez y media prepara su desayuno de leche con Cola Cao y galletas. No toma café.

2 11.00h. A las once practica su música en el estudio.

3 12.30h. Hace ejercicio en el gimnasio a las doce y media.

4 14.00h. A las dos come verduras y carne y para beber, agua.

5 15.30h. ¡Más música! Practica más música a las tres y media de la tarde.

6 17.00h. Nada en la piscina a las cinco con sus amigos.

7 22.00h. Después toma una bebida con sus amigos a las diez de la noche.

Aventura Semanal – ¿Sabes?

El chocolate tiene su origen en Latinoamérica. En 1519 Hernán Cortés, el aventurero español, introduce el chocolate en Europa.

Un desayuno típico de los españoles: un chocolate con churros.

¡Ya sabes!

¿Qué **desayunas**? **Desayuno** leche con cereales.
¿Qué **comes**? **Como** espaguetis.
¿Qué **cenas**? **Ceno** tortilla.
Miguel **desayuna** leche, **come** ensalada y **cena** pizza.

La comida: los cereales, las magdalenas, las tostadas, las galletas, etc.
Tiempo libre: toco la guitarra, bailo, escucho música, escribo cartas, pinto camisetas, duermo la siesta, canto, hablo, etc.

En serio ...

Autoevaluación

Tú, todos los días

1 ¿Qué hora es?
Ejemplo Son las once.

(10 puntos)

2 ¿Qué hora es? Dibuja los relojes en tu cuaderno.
Ejemplo Son las cinco y media.

(5 puntos)

1 Es la una.
2 Son las dos y media.
3 Son las once de la mañana.
4 Son las cuatro y media de la tarde.
5 Son las ocho.

¡no escribas aquí!

3 ¿Qué es? Escribe 5 frases.
Ejemplo Éste es el taller de manualidades.

(10 puntos)

4 Escribe 6 bebidas.

(12 puntos)

5 Escribe 5 comidas.

(10 puntos)

6 Escribe los números en palabras.
Ejemplo 900 = novecientos

(12 puntos)

100   200   500
700   800   1000

7 Escribe el diálogo.

(8 puntos)

¿Quieres?   por favor

8 ¿Te gustan estas cosas? Escribe 5 frases *Sí* y 5 frases *No*.

(20 puntos)

9 ¿Qué haces?
Ejemplo Como tortilla y ensalada.

(4 puntos)

10 ¿Qué hace?
Ejemplo A las dos come.

(9 puntos)

Total =   /100

¡Dos juegos en uno!

Juego 1

- Simplemente sustituye los números por las letras debajo de Juego 2 y descubre las palabras.

Juego 2

- Usa dos dados.
- Tira los dados y di los números y letras en voz alta.
- Sustituye los números por las letras.

¡Nota! Tienes las letras H, Q, D, M.

1		= A/Á
2		= E
3		= I
4		= O/Ó
5		= U
6		= L
7		= C
8		= S
9		= T
10	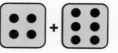	= N
11	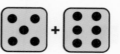	= G
12		= R

¡CANTA LA CANCIÓN!

Quiero un zumo de naranja
una pizza
y un pastel
y coca cola.

Quiero un sandwich
un refresco
un helado
y un café
y coca cola.

Un té con leche
para mi mamá.
Café con leche
para mi papá.

LECCIÓN 16

¿Qué haces?

O B J E T I V O

- *Decir qué haces todos los días.*
- *Decir qué haces el fin de semana.*

A Voy al parque

¿Qué hace Álvaro todos los días? Escucha y mira los dibujos.

1 Voy al parque con mis amigos. **2** Juego en casa. **3** Voy al colegio.

4 Hago mis deberes en casa. **5** Voy al cine. **6** Hago deporte.

Lee y une las frases con los dibujos.

Ejemplo c = 1 Voy al parque con mis amigos.

2 **Estudia.**

El verbo: **ir**   El verbo: **hacer**   El verbo: **jugar**

Goreti **va** al parque.   Raúl **hace** los deberes.   Leticia **juega** a las cartas.

3 **Practica las frases.**

Ejemplo Voy al parque con mis amigos.

	los deberes	en casa.
Voy	al colegio	con mis amigos.
Hago	al parque →	con mis padres.
Juego	al cine	con mis hermanos.
	a la vídeo consola	en el colegio.
	de excursión	
	gimnasia	

Pronunciación

La letra '**v**' en español es como la letra '**b**' en inglés. Escucha y repite.

v = **b** voy, vas, va, vídeo, carnaval

¡Atención!

voy de **excursión** = to go on a trip
el baloncesto = basketball

4 ¿**Qué hace Elena? Escucha y ordena las fotos.**

5 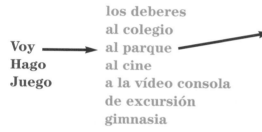 ¿**Y tú? Practica el diálogo con tu compañero(a).**

Ejemplo Estudiante A: ¿Qué haces todos los días? Estudiante B: Voy al colegio, …

Ahora cambia.

B Todos los días

6 Lee la carta de Tessa a Elena. Completa la carta.

Querida Elena:

Todos los _(1) días_ voy al colegio __(2)__ la mañana. Por la _(3)_ voy al centro cultural con mis amigos. Después voy a casa, __(4)__ los deberes o __(5)__ a la vídeo consola. Los _(6)_ de semana voy al cine con mis padres o al parque con mis amigos. __(7)__ domingos descanso en casa y __(8)__ veces voy __(9)__ excursión.

Un abrazo,

Tessa

7 Escucha a Tessa. Compara con la carta.

¿Qué diferencias hay? Corrige la carta.

8 ¿Qué haces tú? Escribe una carta similar a tu amigo(a).

9 Ahora tú. Habla con tu compañero(a).

C ¿Qué actividades hay?

10 Lee los anuncios del Centro Cultural Delicias e indica *Sí* o *No*.

• **Maquillaje.** De febrero a mayo. Lunes y miércoles de 16 a 20 h. 500 ptas./mes.

• **Vídeo.** De febrero a abril. Miércoles y viernes de 19 a 21 h.

• **Pintura.** De febrero a abril. Martes y jueves de 19.30 a 21.30 h. 2.000 ptas./curso.

• **Cerámica.** Febrero y marzo. Lunes y miércoles de 17 a 19 h. 600 ptas./mes.

• **Fotografía.** De febrero a abril. Lunes y jueves de 19 a 21 h. 1.000 ptas./mes.

• **No sexismo.** Febrero. Jueves de 19 a 20.30 h. 600 ptas.

• **Danza africana.** De febrero a abril. Martes y jueves de 14 a 19 h. 1.500 ptas./curso.

1 El curso de **Danza africana** es en mayo. Sí/No
2 Hay un curso de **Pintura** dos días a la semana. Sí/No
3 El curso de **Maquillaje** es 1.000 ptas el mes. Sí/No
4 El curso de **Vídeo** es a las siete de la tarde. Sí/No
5 Hay un curso de **Fotografía** tres días a la semana. Sí/No
6 Hay un curso de **Cerámica** en abril. Sí/No
7 El curso de **No sexismo** es un día a la semana. Sí/No

Encuesta de la clase. Pregunta a tus compañeros(as): ¿Qué haces todos los días?

 Completa el cuadro. Escribe en tu base de datos.

	Todos los días	Los fines de semana	Por las tardes
Estudiante 1	*va al colegio*	*va al cine los sábados*	¡no escribas aquí!
Estudiante 2			
Estudiante 3			
Estudiante 4			

¿Qué actividades son más populares? ¿Y menos?

 Escribe frases sobre cada estudiante. Ejemplo James va al cine los sábados.

Aventura Semanal – ¿Sabes?

También hay juegos de vídeo consola en español.

Éste es un ejemplo de un curso para un estudiante de español.

¿Te gusta estudiar español así?

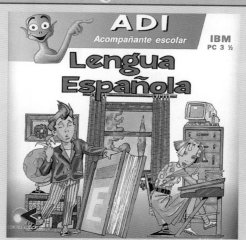

¡Ya sabes!

El verbo: **hacer**
(yo) **hago** deporte.
(tú) **haces** gimnasia
(él/ella) **hace** los deberes.

¿Qué **haces** todos los días?
Hago deporte.

Los actividades: voy al parque, hago los deberes, juego en casa, voy de excursión, etc.
Expresiones de tiempo: todos los días, por la mañana, por la tarde, los fines de semana, los domingos, a veces, etc.

Me gusta jugar al fútbol

- *Decir qué te gusta (y no te gusta) hacer en tu tiempo libre.*
- *Hablar de deportes y juegos.*

A ¿Qué te gusta hacer?

 Escucha y mira las fotos. Tapa las palabras.

1 dibujar

2 jugar a la vídeo consola

3 ir a la piscina

4 patinar

5 hacer los deberes

6 jugar al fútbol

7 ir en bicicleta

8 escuchar música

9 bailar

10 ver la televisión

11 cantar

12 tocar la guitarra

Ahora, une las fotos con las frases.

 Escucha y comprueba.

2 Escucha e indica.

	Jaime	Goreti	Elena
jugar a la vídeo consola			
jugar al fútbol			
hacer los deberes		¡no escribas aquí!	
dibujar			
patinar			

3 Estudia.

¿Te gusta patinar?

Sí, me gusta.

¿Le gusta patinar?

No, no le gusta patinar.

No me gusta patinar.

155

4 Habla con tu compañero(a). Estudiante A: Adopta los gustos de Jaime, Goreti o Elena. Estudiante B: Adivina quién es.

Continúa.

Ahora escribe frases. **Ejemplo** Jaime: Me gusta jugar al fútbol.

5 Lee la carta de Leticia. ¿Qué le gusta? ¿Qué no le gusta?

Querido Raúl:
Me gusta patinar, me gusta jugar a la vídeo consola. No me gusta dibujar pero me gusta bailar y cantar. También me gusta tocar el piano. No me gusta estudiar ni hacer deberes. Me gusta todo tipo de música y ver la televisión.
Un abrazo,

Leticia

 Ahora escucha a Elena. Indica qué es diferente de la carta de Leticia.

Leticia	Elena
Me gusta patinar	Me gusta ...

6 Escribe una carta a un(a) amigo(a) sobre qué te gusta y no te gusta.

7 Mira las fotos de Actividad 1 y habla con tus compañeros(as).

Ejemplo Estudiante A: ¿Qué te gusta hacer? Estudiante B: Me gusta jugar al fútbol.

¿Qué actividades son más populares en la clase? Escribe los resultados en la base de datos de la clase.

B Los deportes

8 **Mira los dibujos, escucha y repite.**

a el fútbol   **b** el baloncesto   **c** el atletismo   **d** la natación

e el tenis   **f** el voleibol   **g** el ping-pong

Ahora une el nombre con el dibujo.

9 **Escucha a Tessa. Habla de sus amigos(as). ¿Qué deportes les gustan (✔) y qué deportes no les gustan (✗)?**

	Cristian	Sara	Carlos
fútbol			
baloncesto			
tenis			

¡no escribas aquí!

C Los resultados

10 **Escucha y escribe los resultados en el cuadro.**

I	Real Celta	I	Real Betis	2
2	Deportivo Coruña		Real Madrid	
3	Barcelona		Logroñés	
4	Real Valladolid		Albacete	
5	Real Oviedo		Athletic Bilbao	
6	Real Sociedad		Sporting Gijón	
7	Tenerife		Racing Santander	
8	Valencia		Español	
9	Atlético Madrid		Compostela	
10	Sevilla		Real Zaragoza	

¡no escribas aquí!

La selección nacional española de fútbol mundial 1994.

11  **En España hay muchos deportes con nombres similares al inglés. Escucha.**

fútbol béisbol **voleibol**

tenis bádminton **rugby**

judo hockey esquí

atletismo boxeo

También hay otros deportes muy populares en España. Escucha.

hockey patines

pelota

balonmano

Aventura Semanal

Me gusta el fútbol

Me gusta el fútbol
también la natación.
Me gusta el tenis
el hockey y el ping-pong.

Me gusta el rugby
me gusta el voleibol.
Me gusta el baloncesto
mi equipo es Campeón.

La canción

¡Ya sabes!

¿Qué **te gusta hacer**?
Me gusta jugar al fútbol.

No **me gusta hacer** los deberes.
(No) le gusta el fútbol.

Vocabulario del tiempo libre: ver la televisión, leer, jugar, escuchar música, etc.
Los deportes: el fútbol, el baloncesto, la natación, el rugby, el voleibol, el atletismo, etc.

¿Quieres ir al cine?

- *Aceptar y rechazar invitaciones.*   - *Hablar de cine.*

A ¿Quieres ir al cine?

1  **Escucha y lee los diálogos.**

¿Quieres ir a la piscina?

No. No me gusta la piscina.

¿Quieres ir al cine?

Sí, bueno.

2 **Estudia.**

Invitaciones:			
¿Quieres	ir	al cine?	Quiero...
	venir?		
	jugar	conmigo?	
	salir?		
	ver	una película?	

 154

¡Atención!

bueno = OK
vale = OK

salir = to go out
venir = to come

conmigo = with me
contigo = with you

3 Ahora tú. Usa las fotos y habla con tu compañero(a).
Estudiante A: Invita a estudiante B. Estudiante B: Responde.

Ejemplo Estudiante A: ¿Quieres jugar al fútbol? Estudiante B: No. No me gusta el fútbol.

patinar

jugar a la
vídeo consola

jugar al fútbol

ir en bicicleta

jugar al tenis

ir a la piscina

jugar a las cartas

ir a la discoteca

B Una película de aventuras

4 ¿Quieres ir al cine conmigo? Escucha.

1 una película romántica

2 una película cómica

3 una película de ciencia ficción

4 una película de aventuras

5 una película de terror

6 una película policiaca

7 una película de
dibujos animados

8 una película de guerra

9 una película del oeste

Ahora une las palabras con las películas.

5   ¿Qué películas son las favoritas de la clase? Encuesta.

Ejemplo Estudiante A: ¿Te gustan las películas cómicas?
         Estudiante B: Sí, me gustan mucho./No, no me gustan.

Escribe los resultados en la base de datos.

6   Pedro invita a María al cine. ¿Qué películas les gustan y no les gustan? Escucha el diálogo. Después practica el diálogo con tu compañero(a).   Cambia.

¿Quieres ver una película de terror?

No. No me gustan las películas de terror.

C Dos entradas, por favor

7   Escucha los números y repite.

1000   2000   3000   4000   5000

8   Escucha y mira el dibujo.

Dos entradas, por favor.

Toma.

¿Cuánto es?

Mil pesetas.

¡Atención!

1000 = mil
2000 = dos mil
3000 = tres mil
4000 = cuatro mil
5000 = cinco mil

9   Habla con tu compañero(a). Estudiante A: Compra las entradas.
    Estudiante B: Di cuánto es.   Cambia.

1

2

3

10 **Lee la entrevista con Carlos y mira las fotos. Completa la información de los datos personales de Carlos.**

Carlos es un chico con mucho talento. Le gusta ir en su mountain bike, le gusta mucho el monopatín y el snowboard, y forma parte de un grupo musical. Carlos es el vocalista y toca la guitarra, la batería y el bajo.

DATOS PERSONALES

Nombre: *Carlos*
Años: *17*
De: *Málaga*
Signo: *Capricornio*
Estatura: *1,83 m.*
Color de ojos: *Azul*
Le gusta: *Música, naturalidad, chicas sinceras* y _____
Profesión: *Estudiante* y _____

¡no escribas aquí!

Aventura Semanal – ¿Sabes?

España es un país muy popular para hacer películas. En Almería, en Andalucía, hacen películas del oeste. En Tenerife hacen películas de ciencia ficción y en Belchite, en Aragón, hacen películas de guerra.

¡Ya sabes!

¿**Quieres ir** al cine?
Quiero ver una película de aventuras.

Dos entradas, por favor.
Toma.

¿Quieres jugar **conmigo**?
No. No quiero jugar **contigo**.

Tipos de películas: una película de aventuras, de terror, de ciencia ficción, del oeste, una película cómica, romántica, etc.
Los números: 1000, 2000, 3000, 4000, 5000.

El equipo del campamento

● *Decir qué necesitas para ir de camping.*

● *Comprar las cosas necesarias.*

A El equipo del campamento

I ¿Qué cosas necesitas en el campamento? Escucha.

a un plato

b una mochila

c un saco de dormir

d un mapa

e una gorra

f un bronceador

g unas botas

h un cepillo de dientes

i papel

j una linterna

k unas tiritas

l un bolígrafo

m unas zapatillas de deporte

 Ahora lee y une las palabras con los dibujos.

 Escucha y comprueba.

Singular	Plural
un plato = one plate	**unos** platos = some plates
una tirita = one plaster	**unas** tiritas = some plasters

 144

¡Atención!

necesitar = to need
la tienda = the shop
la cosa = the thing

2 Tessa describe la mochila de su amiga. ¿Qué mochila es?

Mercedes

1

2

3

3 Estudiante A: Elige una mochila (Actividad 2) y explica a tu compañero(a) los objetos que tienes en la mochila.
Estudiante B: Adivina qué mochila es.

Ejemplo Estudiante A: Tengo un cepillo de dientes, una linterna, ...

Pronunciación

In Spanish 'll' is similar to the 'y' sound in yellow.

Escucha y repite.

ll   cepillo, llamar
l   mochila, bolígrafo, linterna

B ¿Dónde compras las cosas?

4 Indica en qué tiendas compras las cosas de Actividad 1.

La tienda de camping

La zapatería

La librería

La farmacia

Escucha y comprueba.

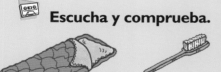

5 ¿Qué más compras en estas tiendas? Escribe una lista.

6 Mira la información del campamento y escucha. ¿Qué equipo necesitas?

Equipo necesario: Necesito ...

una gorra
una cantimplora

un anorak

una linterna

una bolsa de aseo
      con champú
un cepillo de dientes
pasta de dientes
unas tiritas
jabón
un bronceador

un plato
una taza

un cuaderno
un bolígrafo
un libro para leer

unas botas
unas zapatillas
   de deporte

7 Tessa va a las tiendas a comprar las cosas necesarias para el campamento. Escucha.

1 ¿En qué tienda está?
2 ¿Qué compra?

| **a** | **La farmacia** | **b** | **La tienda de camping** |

| **c** | **La librería** | **d** | **La zapatería** |

> **¡Atención!**
>
> **el dependiente** = shop assistant (man)
> **la dependienta** = shop assistant (woman)

8 Une los números con las palabras.

a	110	1	quinientos cincuenta
b	220	2	mil cien
c	440	3	cuatrocientos cuarenta
d	550	4	ciento diez
e	880	5	siete mil setecientos
f	1100	6	ochocientos ochenta
g	3300	7	doscientos veinte
h	5500	8	cinco mil quinientos
i	7700	9	tres mil trescientos

Escucha y comprueba.

9 Escucha y une las cosas con los precios.

1	la mochila	a	350ptas
2	las botas	b	5300ptas
3	el anorak	c	250ptas
4	el libro	d	650ptas
5	el bronceador	e	850ptas
6	el cepillo de dientes	f	6400ptas
7	el plato y la taza	g	5500ptas
8	las tiritas	h	950ptas

10 **Estás en la tienda. Practica con tu compañero(a).**

Ejemplo Estudiante A: ¿Qué quiere(s)?
Estudiante B: Quiero un(a) ... (etc.). ¿Cuánto es?
Estudiante A: Son ... pesetas.

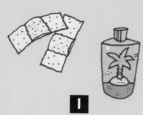
1

2

3

4

Ahora cambia.

C De excursión

11 **En grupo. Vas de excursión para unos días. Elige cinco cosas importantes. Escribe las cosas en órden. Decide. ¿Cuál es la cosa más importante? Compara con tus compañeros(as).**

Ejemplo Necesito una linterna, ...

Aventura Semanal – ¿Sabes?

El camping y el ciclismo son muy populares en España. A los chicos y chicas españoles les gusta la aventura. Una marca de cereales ofrece regalos para las vacaciones. Mira el anuncio.

¡Ya sabes!	
El verbo: **necesitar** (yo) **necesito** (tú) **necesitas** (él/ella) **necesita**	Quiero **un** plato, **una** mochila, **unos** pantalones, **unas** botas, **unas** tiritas. Los números: 110, 220, ..., 4400, 5500. Vocabulario de camping: un saco de dormir, un anorak, unas botas, una linterna, una cantimplora, etc.

Ropa de invierno: ropa de verano

● *Hablar de tu ropa.*

A ¿Qué ropa tienes?

Escucha y mira los dibujos. Repite.

la falda

el pantalón

el vestido

la chaqueta

el abrigo

la camiseta

la camisa

el pantalón corto

el anorak

el jersey

el chándal

los pantalones vaqueros

2 **¿Qué ropa tienen? Escucha a los chicos y las chicas y completa el cuadro.**

	Leticia	Goreti	Jaime	Iñigo
falda				
pantalón				
jersey				
chaqueta				

¡no escribas aquí!

¿Qué ropa es más popular?

3 **Mira la ropa de Actividad 1. Escribe una lista de ropa de invierno y una lista de ropa de verano.**

¡Atención!

la primavera = spring
el verano = summer
el otoño = autumn
el invierno = winter

B ¿Llevas uniforme?

4 **Lee la carta de Sara.**   **Contesta las preguntas:**

Querida Tessa:

Me preguntas si llevo uniforme. En muchos colegios españoles no hay uniforme, pero en mi colegio sí hay. Las chicas llevamos una falda roja y azul oscura de cuadros y jersey azul oscuro. Los chicos llevan pantalones grises. Llevamos zapatos negros y medias o calcetines negros o azules. No me gusta llevar uniforme pero es obligatorio. No tengo una foto con uniforme pero te envío un dibujo. ¿Y tú? ¿Llevas uniforme? ¿Cómo es? Mándame una foto. Un abrazo fuerte,

Sara

1 ¿Qué dibujo es el uniforme de Sara?
2 ¿Los colegios españoles llevan uniforme?
3 ¿Le gusta llevar uniforme?
4 ¿Cómo es el uniforme de los chicos?

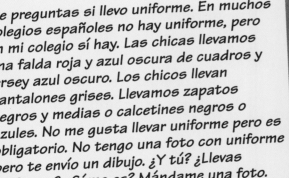

El verbo: llevar

The verb **llevar** has two meanings:

1. to wear (clothes)

2. to carry (something)

(yo) **llevo** - I wear/carry

(tú) **llevas** - you ...

(él/ella) **lleva** - he/she ...

152

¡Atención!

de cuadros = chequered
los calcetines = socks
las medias = tights
la camiseta = T-shirt
                     or vest

5   Mira los uniformes del colegio de Tessa.

una corbata negra

un jersey negro

una camisa blanca

una chaqueta negra

un pantalón negro

una falda blanca y negra

medias negras

zapatos negros

   Lee y completa la carta de Tessa.

En mi colegio llevamos _____ . Es muy
bonito y me gusta mucho. Llevamos una
_____ negra, una _____ blanca, una
_____ negra y un _____ negro. Los
chicos y las chicas llevan un _____
negro. Las chicas llevan también una _____
blanca y negra de cuadros con _____
negras. Los _____ son negros.
Para los deportes llevamos
un jersey rojo.

¡no escribas aquí!

6   ¿Y tú? ¿Llevas uniforme? Escribe una
carta a un(a) amigo(a). Dibuja *tu*
uniforme y descríbelo. (Si no llevas
uniforme describe tu ropa típica).

7   Diseña *tu* uniforme o ropa ideal.
Descríbelo a tu compañero(a).

C   **Preparando la ropa del campamento**

8   Mira las fotos de Leticia. ¿Qué lleva en
el invierno? ¿Qué lleva en el verano?
Escribe dos listas.

Ejemplo En el invierno lleva un anorak amarillo, ...

9   Pregunta a tu compañero(a):
¿Qué ropa llevas en el invierno y
en el verano?

10 **La ropa del campamento. Tessa lee la lista de ropa que necesita. Escucha e indica.**

una gorra

dos jerseys
un anorak

ropa interior:
calcetines
bragas
camisetas
pijamas

tres camisas o
blusas
dos pantalones
largos
un pantalón corto
un pantalón vaquero
bañador

botas
zapatos deportivos
sandalias de agua

11 **Tessa y su madre están preparando la mochila. Mira la lista de Actividad 10. Indica qué tiene ✔ y qué no tiene ✗.**

12 **Mira las fotos de los chicos y las chicas del campamento. Describe la ropa de uno(a) a tu compañero(a). ¿Quién es? Tu compañero(a) adivina. Cambia.**

Aventura Semanal

Voy elegante a la fiesta de mi amigo,
llevo camisa y llevo pantalón.

En el invierno yo llevo un abrigo
y en el verano yo llevo bañador.

Hago deporte y llevo camiseta
pantalón corto y gorra para el sol.

La canción

¡Ya sabes!

¿Qué **llevas** en el invierno? **Llevo** abrigo, ...
¿Qué **lleva** en el verano? **Lleva** camiseta, ...

Un jersey rojo, una chaqueta negra.

Vocabulario de ropa: una camisa, un pantalón vaquero (vaqueros), unos calcetines, unas medias, un anorak, etc.

Autoevaluación — Tú y el tiempo libre

I ¿Qué te gusta y no te gusta hacer en tu tiempo libre? Escribe 7 frases.
Ejemplo Me gusta ir al cine.

(14 puntos)

2 Escribe 7 frases con estas palabras:
Ejemplo Voy al parque.

(14 puntos)

hago voy nado

escucho veo juego toco

3 Invita a un(a) amigo(a), completa los diálogos.

(6 puntos)

4 Escribe 7 tipos de películas.

(14 puntos)

5 Escribe estos números en palabras.

(14 puntos)

1500 2000 3350 4000 5900 6400 750

6 Escribe el diálogo.

(4 puntos)

7 Mira los dibujos y escribe los nombres de 6 objetos.

(6 puntos)

8 Escribe los nombres de las tiendas donde compras estas cosas.

(4 puntos)

9 Escribe 8 nombres de ropa.

(8 puntos)

10 Mira la ropa de 9. ¿De qué color es?
Ejemplo La falda es azul, ...

(16 puntos)

Total = /100

... y en broma

Los campeones del deporte español

1 Miguel Induráin, campeón de ciclismo.
2 José María Olazábal, campeón de golf.
3 Martín López Zubero, campeón de natación.
4 Conchita Martínez, campeona de tenis y la primera ganadora española de Wimbledon.

I Escribe los nombres de los deportistas de cada símbolo.

2 ¿Qué ropa llevan? Escribe la ropa que llevan los futbolistas. Mira los deportes de Actividad I. ¿Qué ropa llevan para cada deporte?

1 El ciclismo:
2 El tenis:
3 El golf:
4 El atletismo:
5 La natación:

¡no escribas aquí!

3 Dibuja a *tu* deportista favorito(a) y escribe qué ropa lleva.

De vacaciones

● *Hablar de las vacaciones.*

A ¿Adónde vas de vacaciones?

1 Mira los dibujos y escucha.

1 la montaña
2 la playa
3 el pueblo
4 el campo
5 el extranjero
6 el campamento

a | b | c | d | e | f

Une las palabras con los dibujos.

2 Mira y escucha.

¿Adónde vas de vacaciones?

Voy a la montaña.

Voy al pueblo. ¿Adónde vas tú?

No voy de vacaciones.

3 Escucha a los chicos y chicas e indica adónde van de vacaciones.

	Goreti	Carlos	Elena	Leticia	Cristian
la playa					
la montaña		¡no escribas aquí!			
el campamento					

4 Pregunta a tus compañeros(as): ¿Adónde vas de vacaciones?
Usa los dibujos de Actividad 1.

B ¿Dónde está Pedro?

5 Pedro está en casa. ¿Dónde están los amigos y amigas de Pedro?
Escucha y une los chicos y chicas con los dibujos.

¿Dónde están mis amigos?

Vanessa

Julio

Natalia

Francisco

Goreti

Ahora escribe frases.

Ejemplo Julio está en el pueblo.

6 📼 **Estudia y escucha.**

¡Hola! Soy María.

¡Hola María! ¿Dónde estás?

Estoy en el pueblo.

SOS Gramática SOS

El verbo: **estar** = to be (position)

(yo)   **estoy** = I am
(tú)   **estás** = you are
(él/ella)   **está** = he/she is

➡ 153

7 💬 **Habla con tu compañero(a). Elige un lugar: la piscina, el cine, etc.**

Ejemplo Estudiante A: ¿Dónde estás? Estudiante B: Estoy en el(la) …

        Cambia.

C   ¿Dónde está el campamento?

8 📼 **Hoy Tessa y otros chicos y chicas van al campamento de vacaciones. Tessa habla con su nueva amiga, Pili.**

Escucha a Tessa y a Pili y contesta *Sí* o *No*.

1 Tessa va al campamento todos los años.   Sí/No
2 Pili va al campamento por primera vez.   Sí/No
3 Tessa y Pili son de Zaragoza.   Sí/No
4 Las tiendas de camping son pequeñas.   Sí/No
5 El campamento está en Broto.   Sí/No
6 Broto es un pueblo grande.   Sí/No

¡Atención!

la tienda de camping = tent

cerca (de) = near to
lejos (de) = far from

9 📖 **Estudia.**

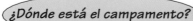

¿Dónde está el campamento?

El campamento está en las montañas. Está en Broto.

10 📖 **Tessa escribe a su amiga Lindsey. Lee la carta y completa con: estoy, está.**

Querida Lindsey:

_____ en un campamento. El campamento ___está___ en las montañas, en los Pirineos de España. _____ cerca de Broto, un pueblo pequeño y muy bonito. _____ cerca de una montaña muy alta que se llama El Mondariego. _____ lejos de Belchite donde viven mis abuelos. El campamento _____ en una pradera y el río _____ cerca.

Hasta luego
Tessa

✏️ **Escribe una frase para cada foto.**

Ejemplo a = El campamento está en los Pirineos.

Aventura Semanal – ¿Sabes?

¿Cómo pasan los niños las vacaciones?

Las vacaciones de verano en España son muy largas, desde junio hasta septiembre: en total tres meses aproximadamente.

En Colombia, los colegios toman las vacaciones en noviembre, diciembre y enero, o en julio y agosto. Los chicos colombianos visitan a los abuelos o van a la playa en Cartagena y otros lugares.

¡Ya sabes!

¿**Adónde vas** de vacaciones?
Voy al campamento.
No voy de vacaciones.

El verbo: **estar**

¿Dónde **estás**?
Estoy en el pueblo.
El campamento **está** cerca de las montañas. **Está** lejos de la playa.

Vocabulario de vacaciones: el pueblo, la playa, el extranjero, las montañas, el campo, etc.

¿Cómo es tu ciudad?

● *Decir de dónde eres.*   ● *Hablar de tu ciudad o tu pueblo.*

A ¿Cómo es tu ciudad?

1 ¿Qué hay en la ciudad? Escucha y mira los dibujos. Tapa las palabras.

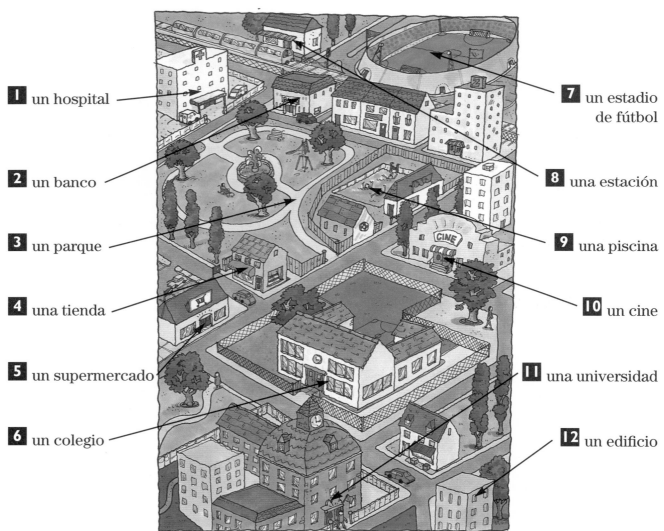

1 un hospital

2 un banco

3 un parque

4 una tienda

5 un supermercado

6 un colegio

7 un estadio de fútbol

8 una estación

9 una piscina

10 un cine

11 una universidad

12 un edificio

 Escucha y comprueba.

2  **Tessa y Pili hablan de la ciudad y del campamento. Escucha.**

	Pili	Tessa
¿Dónde vive?	Barcelona	Londres
¿Cómo es la ciudad?		
¿Prefiere campamento/ciudad?	¡no escribas aquí!	
¿Por qué?		
¿Qué hay?		

3 **¿Y tú? Habla con tu compañero(a). ¿Dónde vives? ¿Cómo es tu ciudad? ¿Qué hay?**

B La ciudad espacial

4 **Pili y Tessa hacen un proyecto en el campamento sobre una ciudad espacial. Lee el artículo y completa el dibujo.**

LA CIUDAD ESPACIAL

En la ciudad hay una estación espacial. Hay un hospital de robots. Hay restaurantes y supermercados modernos. También hay muchos estadios de deportes, de fútbol y de baloncesto y hay piscinas. No hay cines. La gente ve las películas en casa. Hay colegios y profesores pero los estudiantes estudian con los ordenadores y con los robots. Los estudiantes estudian en casa con los ordenadores. Pero sí hay colegios con profesores. Hay parques con árboles de metal y monumentos de plástico.

5 📖 **¿Dónde está? Estudia.**

todo recto   **a la izquierda**   **a la derecha**

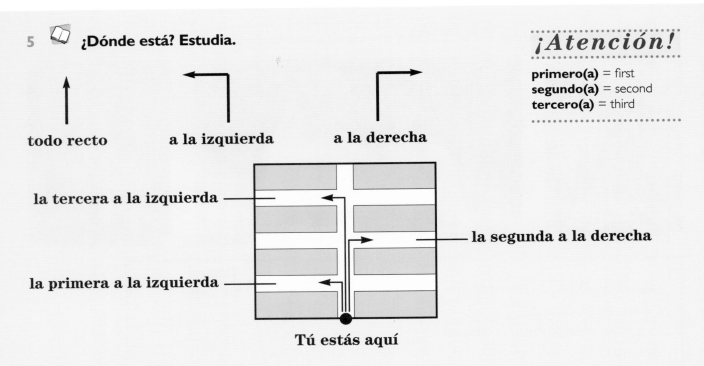

la tercera a la izquierda —

la segunda a la derecha

la primera a la izquierda —

Tú estás aquí

🎧 **Escucha e indica los lugares en el plano: La piscina, el colegio, el estadio de fútbol, el supermercado, el parque y la estación espacial.**

Ejemplo f = la piscina

C ¿Dónde está el campamento?

6 Unos chicos del campamento están de excursión. ¿Pero, dónde están? ¿Dónde está el campamento? Indica el plano correcto.

7 Habla con tu compañero(a). Describe otro de los planos. ¿Cuál es?

8 Envía a un amigo un plano de *tu* zona. Explica dónde están las cosas.

Ejemplo A la derecha está el colegio, ...

Aventura Semanal

¿Dónde está la playa?

Todo recto, todo recto, al final.	Izquierda, derecha, Izquierda, derecha,
Todo recto, todo recto, ¿dónde está?	Delante, detrás, No sé dónde está.

La canción

¡Ya sabes!

¿Cómo es tu ciudad?
Mi ciudad es grande.

¿Qué hay en tu ciudad?
Hay tiendas, edificios, un banco, una universidad, una fábrica, una estación, un estadio de fútbol, etc.

¿Dónde está el campamento?
Todo recto.
La primera a la derecha.
La segunda a la izquierda.
La tercera a la derecha.

¿Cómo es tu casa?

● *Hablar de tu casa.*　　● *Decir dónde están las habitaciones.*

A ¿Cómo es tu casa?

I　Tessa y Pili están en el campamento. Hablan de sus casas en la ciudad.

¿Qué prefieres, la casa o el campamento?

Me gusta el campamento, pero mi casa es muy cómoda

¿Cómo es tu casa?

¡Atención!

una casa = a house
un piso = a flat or a storey

2　Tessa habla de las habitaciones de su casa. Tapa las palabras y escucha.

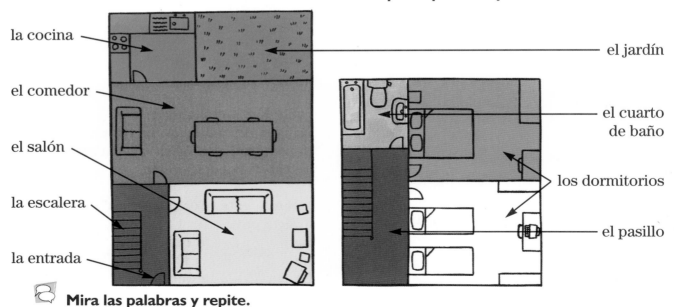

la cocina

el comedor

el salón

la escalera

la entrada

el jardín

el cuarto
de baño

los dormitorios

el pasillo

Mira las palabras y repite.

3 Tatiana habla de su casa. Escucha y ordena las fotos.

B ¿Dónde está Raúl?

4 Mira las fotos de la casa de Raúl. Une las fotos con las frases.

Ésta es la cocina. **a**

Éste es el comedor. **b**

Ésta es la entrada. **c**

Éste es el cuarto de baño. **d**

Ésta es mi casa. **e**

Éste es mi dormitorio. **f**

Éste es el dormitorio de mis padres. **g**

Escucha y comprueba.

5 🗨 **¿Dónde están? Pregunta a tu compañero(a) y cambia.**

Ejemplo Estudiante A: ¿Dónde está Rosita? Estudiante B: Está en el cuarto de baño.

C Al lado de la cocina

6 📼 **Mira los dibujos y escucha.**

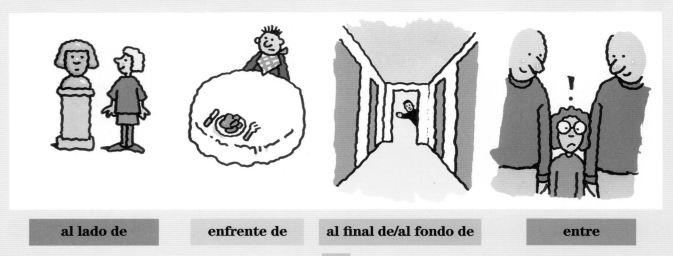

| al lado de | enfrente de | al final de/al fondo de | entre |

7 Jaime envía un plano de su piso con fotos a su amigo. Lee la carta y escribe los nombres de las habitaciones.

Querido Javier:

Éste es un plano de mi nuevo piso. Tiene seis habitaciones. Entras y a la derecha está mi dormitorio. Al lado de mi dormitorio está el salón, la habitación más grande. Enfrente de mi dormitorio está el dormitorio de mis padres. Enfrente del salón está el comedor. La cocina está al fondo del pasillo a la izquierda y el cuarto de baño está a la derecha.
Un abrazo,
Jaime

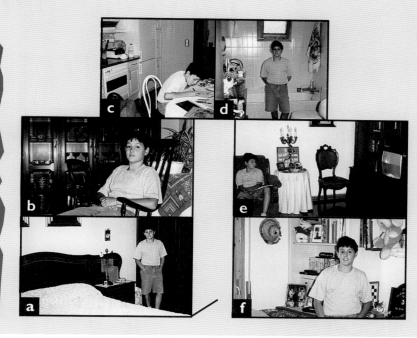

8 Describe tu casa o tu piso a tu compañero(a). Si quieres, ¡inventa!

Aventura Semanal – ¿Sabes?

La arquitectura de Gaudí

Antoni Gaudí (1852-1926) es un famoso arquitecto de Reus. Reus está en el este de España. La arquitectura de Gaudí es muy original. En Barcelona hay casas y monumentos muy interesantes de Gaudí. ¿Te gusta la arquitectura? Mira las fotos.

9 Dibuja *tu* casa ideal y escribe los nombres de las habitaciones.

¡Ya sabes!

¿**Cómo es** tu casa?
Es cómoda.
Tiene seis habitaciones.

¿**Dónde está** el salón?
El salón está **enfrente del** comedor.
Está **entre** el baño y mi dormitorio.
La cocina está **al final del** pasillo.

Vocabulario de la casa: la habitación, el salón, el comedor, la cocina, el cuarto de baño, el dormitorio, el pasillo, la entrada, la escalera, el jardín, etc.

LECCIÓN 24

En el campamento

OBJETIVO

- Describir un campamento.
- Hablar de las actividades del campamento.

A Las tiendas del campamento

 1 Mira los dibujos del campamento y escucha.

1 la cocina

2 la lavandería

3 las duchas

4 los servicios

5 la clínica

6 la tienda de juegos

7 el comedor

8 la tienda de dormir

2 **Joaquín describe el campamento. Une el símbolo con el número de la tienda.**

 Habla con tu compañero(a).

Ejemplo
Estudiante A: ¿Qué tienda es la número siete?
Estudiante B: Es la cocina.

Continúa.

 Escribe una frase para cada tienda.

Ejemplo La tienda número siete es la cocina.

SOS Gramática SOS

nosotros(as)	preparamos	-	we prepare
	comemos	-	we eat
	dormimos	-	we sleep
¡Nota!	**vamos**	-	**we go**

153

3 **Une las frases con las fotos.**

a En esta tienda dormimos.   **b Aquí lavamos la ropa.**

c En esta tienda comemos, desayunamos y cenamos.

d En esta tienda jugamos.

e En esta tienda preparamos la comida.

 Escucha y comprueba.

4 Tessa escribe una carta a sus padres. Lee y completa la carta.

Queridos papás:
El campamento es muy bonito. Hay diez tiendas. A la izquierda, las tiendas número uno a cinco son las tiendas de dormir. Aquí ____(1)____ . Hay espacio para ocho chicos y chicas en cada tienda. La tienda número seis es la cocina y aquí ____(2)____ . La siete es el comedor donde ____(3)____ , ____(4)____ y ____(5)____ . Esta tienda también es la tienda de actividades donde ____(6)____ . Al lado de la tienda de actividades están las duchas y los servicios. La lavandería, donde ____(7)____ está al lado de los servicios. La tienda número diez es la clínica adonde ____(8)____ si tenemos un accidente.
Un abrazo,
Tessa

a lavamos la ropa	**e** preparamos la comida
b dormimos	**f** comemos
c vamos	**g** jugamos
d desayunamos	**h** cenamos

B **¿Dónde están?**

5 Escucha a los chicos y las chicas. ¿Dónde está cada chico(a)? Ejemplo 1 = d

1 ¡No hay agua!

2 ¿Dónde está mi saco de dormir?

3 Preparamos patatas fritas.

4 Lavamos las camisetas.

5 ¡Oh, mi pie!

6 ¿Qué quieres comer?

7 ¿Jugamos a las cartas?

C El campamento y la casa

6 ¿Qué haces en el campamento? ¿Qué haces en tu casa? ¿Qué haces en casa y también en el campamento? Escribe tres listas.

7 Escribe frases.

Ejemplo En casa vemos la televisión.

Aventura Semanal – ¿Sabes?

En las vacaciones muchos chicos y chicas españoles y latinoamericanos van a un campamento durante quince días. En los campamentos hay muchas actividades: deportes, trabajos manuales, excursiones. Es muy interesante y divertido.

En México las vacaciones son en julio y agosto. Muchos chicos mexicanos van a los campamentos en México y los Estados Unidos, o van a las escuelas de verano para estudiar baile, natación o pintura.

Para muchos chicos de la ciudad es la única oportunidad de ir al campo.

¡Y hacen muchos amigos!

¡Ya sabes!

Dormimos en la tienda de dormir.
Comemos en el comedor.
Preparamos la comida en la cocina.
Vamos al parque.

Vocabulario del campamento: la cocina, la lavandería, las duchas, los servicios, la clínica, la tienda de juegos, el comedor, la tienda de dormir, etc.

25

Mi habitación

O B J E T I V O

● **Describir tu habitación.**   ● **Decir dónde están las cosas.**

A Tengo un armario

1 Mira y escucha.

¿Qué tienes en tu habitación en casa?

Tengo una cama, un armario ...

2 Escucha y repite.

Los muebles de mi habitación

el armario

las estanterías

la mesa

la silla

los pósters

la cama

la lámpara

la mesilla

el sillón

3  Jaime, Elena y Raúl describen sus habitaciones. ¿Qué hay?

Jaime

Raúl

Elena

			¡no escribas aquí!		
Jaime					
Raúl					
Elena					

Escribe frases para Jaime, Raúl y Elena.

Ejemplo En la habitación de Elena hay una cama, ...

4 Estudiante A: Describe tu habitación a tu compañero(a).
Estudiante B: Dibuja la habitación.

¿Es correcto? Cambia.

5 ¿Qué tienes en tu habitación? Si quieres, ¡inventa!

Ejemplo En mi habitación tengo una cama, ...

6 Mira las dos habitaciones. ¡Busca siete diferencias!

Ejemplo En la habitación de Héctor el sillón es rojo; en la habitación de Leticia es azul.

7 Lee la carta de Elena. Dibuja su habitación.

¡Hola!

En mi habitación tengo una cama, un armario, una mesa para estudiar y una mesilla al lado de la cama. También hay un sillón enfrente de la cama y delante de una ventana. Las estanterías están al lado de la puerta. La mesilla está entre la mesa y la cama. Tengo pósters en la pared detrás de la silla.
Un abrazo,

Elena

B ¿Dónde está el pantalón?

8 Mira la habitación de Tessa y escucha.

Ejemplo ¿Dónde está el pantalón? El pantalón está en el suelo.

9 ¿Dónde están las cosas? Habla con tu compañero(a).

Ejemplo Estudiante A: ¿Dónde está la cartera?
Estudiante B: Está al lado del armario.

Escribe frases. **Ejemplo** La cartera está al lado del armario.

10 ¿Qué más hay en una casa? Escribe una lista para cada habitación.

Ejemplo La cocina: una mesa, unas sillas, ...

¡Atención!

delante (de) = in front (of)
detrás (de) = behind
encima (de) = above or on top (of)
debajo (de) = below

la pared = the wall
el suelo = floor
los muebles = furniture

C Tu habitación ideal

11 Lee el artículo sobre la casa de José Luis Rodríguez, "El Puma", el famoso cantante venezolano.

"El Puma" vive en el piso 40 de un edificio con una vista fantástica de la playa de Miami. El apartamento es enorme. Tiene siete baños y tres comedores, salones para descansar y salones para ver la televisión o escuchar música. En su casa le gusta la tranquilidad.

Contesta *Sí* o *No*.

1 "El Puma" vive en un apartamento.
2 Tiene muchos cuartos.
3 Está en la montaña.
4 Tiene tres baños y muchos comedores.
5 Le gusta ver la televisión.
6 Escribe una lista de los muebles en las fotos.

Aventura Semanal – ¿Sabes?

Salvador Dalí (1904-89)

Dalí es un pintor muy famoso de Figueras en Cataluña. Sus pinturas son muy interesantes. En el museo Dalí en Figueras, hay una habitación diferente.

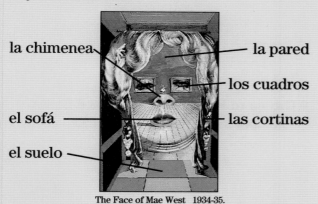

la chimenea — la pared
— los cuadros
el sofá — las cortinas
el suelo —

The Face of Mae West 1934-35.
Photograph © 1994, The Art Institute of Chicago, All Rights Reserved.

12 Juega con tu compañero(a). Usa las fotos del apartamento del Puma.

Ejemplo
Estudiante A: Veo veo.
Estudiante B: ¿Qué ves?
Estudiante A: Una cosa que empieza por A.
Estudiante B: Armario.

Cambia.

13 Dibuja tu habitación ideal. Compara con tus compañeros(as). ¿Qué hay?

¡Ya sabes!

Vocabulario de la habitación: los muebles, un armario, una cama, una mesilla, una lámpara, un sillón, etc.

Posición: Debajo de, encima de, detrás de, delante de, en el suelo, etc.

En serio ...

Autoevaluación Tú y tu mundo

1 ¿Adónde vas de vacaciones?

(8 puntos)

2 ¿Dónde estás?

(6 puntos)

3 ¿Qué hay en la ciudad? Escribe 8 cosas.

(16 puntos)

4 Contesta estas preguntas con frases completas:

(6 puntos)

¡no escribas aquí!

1 ¿Dónde vives?
2 ¿Cómo es tu ciudad?
3 ¿Qué hay en tu ciudad?

5 Mira el plano. Estás en la estación.
Ejemplo ¿Dónde está el número uno?
Todo recto, la primera a la izquierda.

(12 puntos)

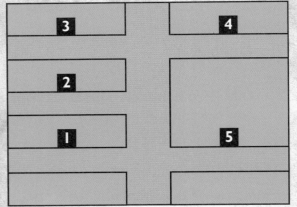

Estación

1 ¿Dónde está el número 2?
2 ¿Dónde está el número 3?
3 ¿Dónde está el número 4?
4 ¿Dónde está el número 5?

6 Escribe 8 lugares de la casa.

(16 puntos)

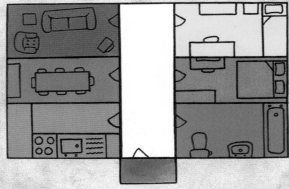

7 ¿Dónde están las habitaciones?

Escribe 8 frases.

Ejemplo El salón está al lado del comedor.

(16 puntos)

8 Une las frases.

(4 puntos)

1 En el dormitorio   a preparamos la comida.
2 En la cocina   b vemos la televisión.
3 En el comedor   c dormimos.
4 En el salón   d cenamos.

9 Completa las frases:
Ejemplo <u>Dormimos</u> en el dormitorio.

(8 puntos)

1 _____ al fútbol.
2 _____ en el comedor.
3 _____ la comida.
4 _____ a la piscina.

10 Dibuja *tu* habitación. Escribe 4 frases.
Ejemplo La mesilla está al lado de la cama.

(8 puntos)

Total /100

E

... y en broma

1 📖 **Mira el dibujo y lee las frases.**

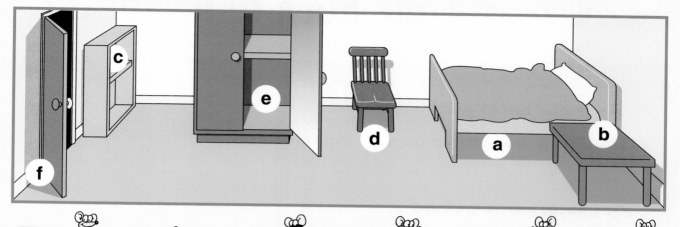

Lleva al ratón a la habitación.

El ratón rojo está debajo de la cama.
El ratón verde está en la estantería.
El ratón negro está delante de la silla.
El ratón azul está dentro del armario.
El ratón amarillo está encima de la mesa.
El ratón blanco está detrás de la puerta.

2 **Mira los dibujos de la ciudad del oeste Tejita. Encuentra las diferencias con tu compañero(a). ¡Di en voz alta las diferencias!**

3 **Lee el poema. Escucha y aprende.**

Luna, lunera
Cascabelera
Debajo de la cama
Tienes la cena

LECCIÓN
26

¿A qué hora te levantas?

O B J E T I V O

- Decir qué haces por las mañanas.
- Hablar de las actividades del campamento.

A ¿Qué haces por la mañana?

1   Mira los dibujos. Escucha y repite. Une las palabras con los dibujos.

a   b   c   d

e   f   g   h

1 me lavo los dientes   **2** me ducho   **3** me visto   **4** me despierto

5 me lavo   **6** me peino   **7** me baño   **8** me levanto

Escucha y comprueba.

2   ¿Qué haces cada mañana? Escribe las frases de Actividad 1 en orden.

Ejemplo Me levanto a las ocho, ...

Compara con tu compañero(a).

Escucha a Héctor y compara con tu lista.

3   Habla con tu compañero(a). Pregunta: ¿A qué hora te levantas? ¿Te bañas o te duchas? ...

Cambia.

122

ciento veintidós

Los verbos reflexivos

levantarse = to get up	ducharse = to shower	¡Nota! vestirse (irregular) = to dress
(yo) **me** levanto	**me** ducho	**me** visto
(tú) **te** levantas	**te** duchas	**te** vistes
(él/ella) **se** levanta	**se** ducha	**se** viste

 147

4 **Ahora tú. ¿Qué haces cada día?**
¡Explica a tu compañero(a) con acciones!

Ejemplo Estudiante A: Dice una acción: Me lavo.
Estudiante B: Mima la acción.
Estudiante A: Sí o No.

B Un día en el campamento

5 **Escucha a Tessa. Explica el horario del campamento.**

EL HORARIO DEL CAMPAMENTO

Actividades
levantarse
hacer gimnasia
lavarse
desayunar
hacer las tareas del día
ducharse
ir de excursión ⎫
hacer actividades ⎬
bañarse en la piscina ⎭
comer
dormir la siesta
hacer actividades ⎫
deportes ⎬
trabajos manuales ⎭
tomar la merienda
jugar ⎫
cantar ⎬
escribir cartas ⎭
cenar
acostarse

¡no escribas aquí!

 Completa el horario.

 Tú eres Oscar o Tessa.
Habla con tus compañeros(as).
¿Qué haces en el campamento?

Ejemplos
Estudiante A: ¿Qué haces a las ocho y media de la mañana?
Estudiante B: Me lavo.

Estudiante A: ¿A qué hora te levantas?
Estudiante B: A las ocho.

Cambia.

6 ✎ **Escribe frases y la hora para cada foto. Ejemplo** Me lavo a las ocho y media.

C Las tareas del campamento

7 📼 **¿Qué tareas haces en el campamento cada día? Escucha a Oscar.**

a Preparo la comida.
b Arreglo mis cosas.
c Lavo los platos.
d Limpio la tienda.
e Lavo la ropa.
f Preparo la mesa.

¡Atención!

la tarea = duty, chore
acostarse = to go to bed
(**me acuesto** a las diez)

📖 **Lee y une las frases con las fotos.**

8 **En el campamento los chicos y chicas hacen tareas en grupos. Escucha a la monitora. Une los grupos con las tareas.**

Grupo A   *Grupo B*   Grupo C

arreglar = to tidy up
limpiar = to clean
ayudar = to help

9 **Lee la carta de Oscar a sus padres. Explica las tareas de su grupo. ¿Qué grupo es?**

Queridos padres:
Hago muchas actividades en el campamento. También cada grupo tiene tareas cada día. Por la mañana me levanto a las ocho. Me lavo, desayuno y preparo las cosas del día. Esta semana mi grupo limpia la tienda de actividades y también lava la ropa.
Un abrazo,
Oscar

10 **¿Y tú? ¿Ayudas en casa? ¿Lavas los platos? ¿Arreglas tus cosas? Habla con tu compañero(a).**

11 **Escribe una carta a Oscar. Explica qué haces en casa.**

Aventura Semanal

Todos los días igual

Todos los días igual
Me despierto
Me levanto
Me ducho o me baño
Desayuno cereales
y para el colegio salgo

Pero hoy es diferente
Tengo clase de español
Hoy tenemos **aventura**
Esta clase es la mejor

 La canción

¡Ya sabes!

Verbos reflexivos:
¿**Te** duchas o te bañas?
Me ducho.
Héctor **se** ducha.

Por la mañana: me despierto, me levanto, me lavo, me ducho, me visto, me peino, me baño, etc.
Las tareas: preparo la comida, arreglo mis cosas, limpio la tienda, lavo la ropa, preparo la mesa, etc.

El tiempo

● *Hablar del tiempo.*

A ¿Qué tiempo hace hoy?

I  **Escucha y repite.**

a Hace calor.

e Hace fresco.

b Hace frío.

f Llueve.

c Hace sol.

g Nieva.

d Hace viento.

h Hay tormenta.

Ahora lee las frases. Une las frases con los dibujos.

2 **¿Qué tiempo hace hoy? Escucha a Oscar.**

3 **Mira los dibujos de Actividad 2 y habla con tu compañero(a). ¿Qué dibujo es?**

Ejemplo Estudiante A: Hace sol y hace calor.
Estudiante B: El número uno.

Cambia.

> **¡Atención!**
>
> **hace frío** = it's cold
> **hace fresco** = it's cool
> **el grado** = degree of temperature

Ahora escribe frases. Ejemplo 1 = Hace calor y hace sol.

4 **Hoy vas a los Pirineos. Escucha el programa y mira los mapas del tiempo. ¿Qué mapa es el de hoy?**

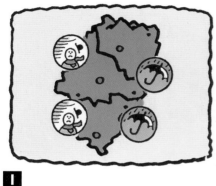

1

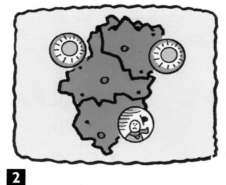

2

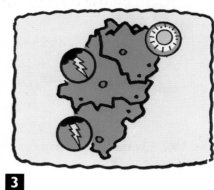

3

Habla con tu compañero(a) del tiempo en los otros dos mapas.

B Las temperaturas

5 **Indica las temperaturas en el mapa de España.**

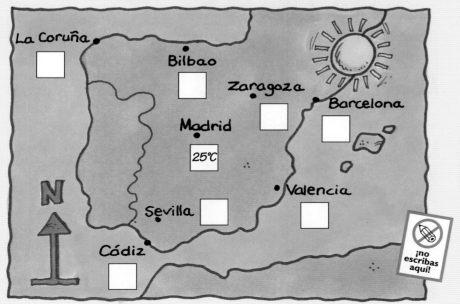

6 Oscar escribe una carta desde el campamento a su amigo Javier. Completa la carta con las frases.

Querido Javier:
Te escribo desde el campamento. Me gusta todo y el tiempo es fantástico. Cuando me levanto a las ocho de la mañana no hace frío pero __(1)__ . A mediodía __(2)__ y por la tarde __(3)__ y me baño en el río. Por la noche necesitamos un saco de dormir porque __(4)__ , a veces la temperatura es de diez grados. A veces __(5)__ muy grandes, pero no __(6)__ mucho.
Un abrazo,
Oscar

¡no escribas aquí!

a hace mucho calor

b hay tormentas

c hace fresco

d hace calor

e hace frío

f llueve

 Escucha y comprueba.

7 Contesta la carta de Oscar. ¿Qué tiempo hace hoy?

8 ¿Qué tiempo hace en estos sitios? Habla con tus compañeros(as).

1

2

3

4

5

6

C ¿Qué haces cuando llueve?

9 Lee las postales. Une las postales con las fotos.

1 Hace mucho calor y mucho sol. Es fantástico. Me gusta mucho la playa. Nado y tomo el sol.

3 Aquí hace sol pero hace mucho frío.Voy a esquiar todos los días. Por las noches voy a las discotecas.

2 Llueve mucho y hace mucho viento, pero vamos a muchas discotecas y cines. Es estupendo.

4 Hace fresco pero hace sol. Vamos de excursión al campo. Hay muchas flores.

10 ¿Qué haces el domingo cuando llueve y hace frío? ¿Qué haces cuando hace sol y hace calor? Pregunta a tu compañero(a).

Aventura Semanal – ¿Sabes?

En Argentina la gente celebra la Navidad en la playa. En diciembre hace calor. Pero en el sur de Argentina, en Patagonia, hace mucho frío todo el año.

En Guatemala llueve mucho entre mayo y octubre. No llueve entre noviembre y abril. No hay verano y no hay invierno. No hace frío.

En el centro de España hace calor en el verano y mucho frío en el invierno.

¡Ya sabes!

¿Qué tiempo hace hoy?
¿Qué haces cuando llueve?

El tiempo: Hace frío, hace calor, hace fresco, hace viento, hace sol, hay tormentas, llueve, nieva, etc.

De excursión

OBJETIVO

● *Describir qué haces de excursión.*

A Vamos de excursión

1 El monitor describe qué hacen en la excursión. Escucha y repite.

Une las frases. Ejemplo 1 = f

1 estudiamos	**a** un bocadillo
2 cruzamos	**b** a la montaña
3 subimos	**c** en el río
4 descansamos	**d** al campamento
5 nos bañamos	**e** el río
6 merendamos	**f** las plantas
7 llegamos	**g** del campamento
8 salimos	**h** de la montaña
9 bajamos	**i** en el pueblo

¡Atención!

un bosque = a wood

en punto = precisely (time)
durar = lasts for (time)

 Escucha y comprueba.

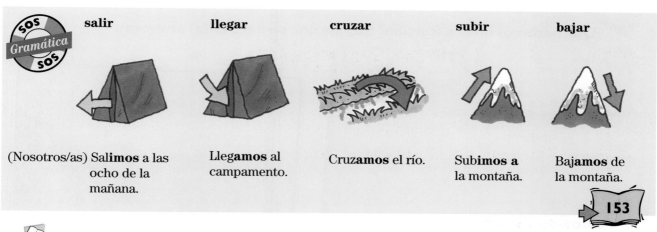

SOS Gramática **SOS**

salir	llegar	cruzar	subir	bajar

(Nosotros/as) Sal**imos** a las ocho de la mañana.

Lleg**amos** al campamento.

Cruz**amos** el río.

Sub**imos a** la montaña.

Baj**amos** de la montaña.

153

2 Lee el programa de la excursión. Mira los mapas e indica el mapa correcto.

EXCURSIÓN AL MONDARIEGO

1 Salir a las ocho y media de la mañana en punto.
2 Subir a la montaña de 1.800 metros que se llama el Mondariego.
3 Ir a un bosque y al río Ara. En el río bañarse, estudiar las plantas y comer.
4 Ir a Buesa, un pueblo. Descansar.
5 Bajar. Cruzar el río.
6 Llegar al campamento a las ocho y media de la tarde. La excursión dura doce horas.

¡Importante! Llevar la comida, agua, y el bañador en la mochila.

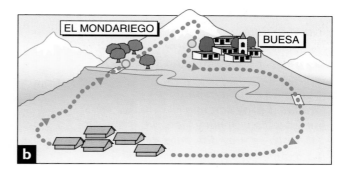

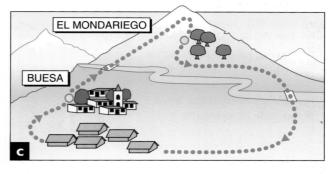

Pronunciación

La letra '**z**' en España se pronuncia como '**th**' en inglés.
En muchos países de Latinoamérica y en el sur de España se pronuncia como la letra '**s**' en inglés. Escucha.

cruzar   plaza   die**z**   **z**apato

3 Habla con tu compañero(a).
     Estudiante A: Mira los tres mapas de Actividad 2 y describe uno a tu compañero(a).
     Estudiante B: Adivina qué mapa es.

4 ✏️ **¿Qué hacemos en la excursión? Escribe una postal a un(a) amigo(a).**

¡Hola!

Vamos de excursión el domingo ...

B El centro de aventuras de Pendarren

5 📖 **El año pasado Tessa fue a Pendarren, un centro de aventuras en Gales. Lee la carta de Tessa a Raúl desde Pendarren. Indica un número para cada foto.**

Querido Raúl,
Te escribo desde Pendarren, en Gales. Es un centro de aventuras.
Estamos en una casa muy grande. Estoy con mis amigas Cloe, Sonia y Victoria (1). Esto es muy diferente del campamento en Broto.
Aquí hace frío y llueve mucho.
Vamos de excursión, vamos en bicicleta, jugamos al fútbol (2), escalamos en la montaña, vamos en piragua.
Hay muchos animales, vacas (3), cerdos, ovejas (4).
Pendarren está cerca de la playa y de la montaña.
Estudiamos las plantas de la playa (5). La comida es muy buena.
Hasta luego,
Tessa

6 Lee las frases e indica Broto, Pendarren o los dos.

	B	P	B/P
1 Hace calor y hace sol.	✔	✘	
2 Vamos de excursión.			
3 Estudiamos las plantas de la playa.			
4 Dormimos en las tiendas.			
5 Nos bañamos en el río.			
6 Estamos en una casa.		¡no escribas aquí!	
7 Estamos cerca de la montaña.			
8 Jugamos en el campo.			
9 Vamos en piragua.			
10 Vamos en bicicleta.			

Aventura Semanal – ¿Sabes?

En los Pirineos hay muchas clases de animales. Hay buitres, águilas y chovas, hay sarrios y bucardos. Hay flores como el edelweis y muchos árboles como pinos, hayas y abetos.

Buitre negro
Águila real
Chova piquirroja
Sarrio
Haya
Edelweiss
Bucardo

7 Habla con tu compañero(a). Mira las fotos y compara los dos campamentos.
   Estudiante A: Habla de Broto.
   Estudiante B: Habla de Pendarren.

Ejemplo Estudiante A: En el campamento de Broto hay tiendas.
   Estudiante B: Pendarren es una casa.

¡Ya sabes!

Vocabulario de excursión: estudiamos las plantas, merendamos un bocadillo, llegamos al campamento, etc.

Los verbos en -ar
nosotros (as)   **cruzamos** el río.
   bajamos de la montaña.
   descansamos en el pueblo.

Los verbos en -er
nosotros(as)   **comemos** un bocadillo.

Los verbos en -ir
nosotros(as)   **salimos** del campamento.
   subimos a la montaña.

LECCIÓN 29

¿Qué tal estás?

A ¿Qué tal estás?

1 Escucha y une los dibujos con las frases.

a   b   c

1 Estoy regular.

2 Estoy mal.

3 Estoy bien.

2 Pregunta a tus compañeros(as): ¿Qué tal estás?

3 Mira los dibujos y tapa las palabras. Escucha y repite. Une las frases con los dibujos.

1   2   3

4   5   6

a Estoy triste.

b Estoy cansado.

c Estoy enfadada.

d Estoy enfermo.

e Estoy aburrida.

f Estoy contenta.

Escucha y comprueba.

Masculino	Femenino
Estoy aburrido.	Estoy aburrida.
Estás cansado.	Estás cansada.
Está triste.	Está triste.

154

4 **Juega a las familias.**

La familia aburrida

Antonio Aburrido (el padre)

La familia enfadada

Pepa Enfadada (la madre)

La familia contenta

Luisito Contento (el hijo)

La familia triste

Juanita Triste (la hija)

B Me duele la cabeza

5 **Mira el dibujo del cuerpo. Escucha y repite.**

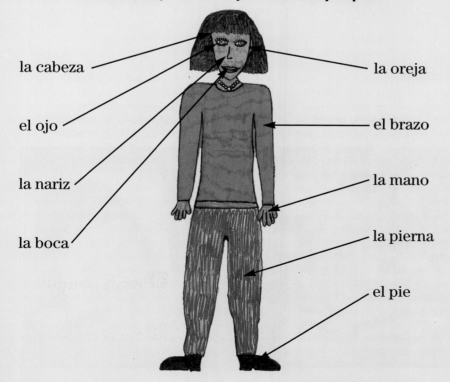

la cabeza

la oreja

el ojo

el brazo

la nariz

la mano

la boca

la pierna

el pie

¡Atención!

el cuerpo = the body
el diente = the tooth
los dientes = teeth
las manos = hands
los ojos = eyes
las orejas = ears
los brazos = arms
las piernas = legs
los pies = feet

6   Mira el dibujo. Escribe los nombres del cuerpo.

7   Escucha las instrucciones. ¡Dibuja el monstruo!

8   Estudiante A: Dibuja un monstruo y
describelo a tu compañero(a).
Estudiante B: Dibuja el monstruo. Compara.
Cambia.

9   ¡Canta la canción!

Al corro la patata
que muy bonito es
un pie, otro pie
una mano, otra mano
un brazo, otro brazo
una pierna, otra pierna
un ojo, otro ojo
un codo, otro codo
la nariz y el gorro.

C   ¿Qué te pasa?

10   Escucha a estos chicos y chicas.

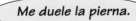

Me duele la pierna.

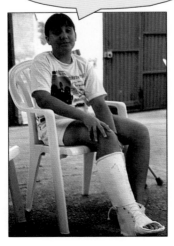

Me duele el pie.

Me duele la cabeza.

11 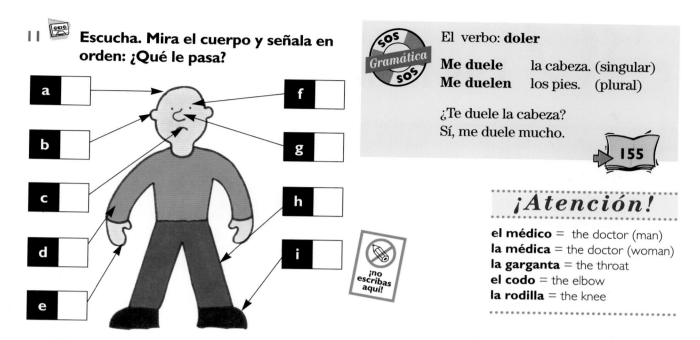 **Escucha. Mira el cuerpo y señala en orden: ¿Qué le pasa?**

a
b
c
d
e
f
g
h
i

¡no escribas aquí!

SOS Gramática SOS

El verbo: **doler**

Me duele la cabeza. (singular)
Me duelen los pies. (plural)

¿Te duele la cabeza?
Sí, me duele mucho.

155

¡*Atención!*

el médico = the doctor (man)
la médica = the doctor (woman)
la garganta = the throat
el codo = the elbow
la rodilla = the knee

12 **Habla con tu compañero(a). Tu compañero(a) es el(la) médico(a). Inventa diálogos similares.**
Ejemplo Estudiante A: ¿Qué te pasa? Estudiante B: Me duele ...

Aventura Semanal

A mi burro, a mi burro
le duele la cabeza
y el médico le manda
una gorrita nueva.
Una gorrita nueva
mi burro enfermo está.

A mi burro, a mi burro
le duele la garganta
y el médico le manda
una bufanda blanca.
Una bufanda blanca
mi burro enfermo está.

La canción

¡Ya sabes!

El verbo: **doler**
Me duele la cabeza.
Me duelen los ojos.
¿**Te duele** el pie?

¿Qué te pasa? ¿Qué tal estás?
Estoy bien, regular, mal, triste, enfermo(a),
aburrido(a), cansado(a), contento(a), enfadado(a).

Vocabulario del cuerpo: la cabeza, la nariz, los
brazos, las piernas, los ojos, las manos, los pies, etc.

30 Las fiestas

OBJETIVO

- *Hablar de fiestas y diversiones.*
- *Decir qué te gusta de las fiestas.*

A ¡Vamos a la fiesta!

1 Escucha a las chicos y chicas.

> ¡Vamos a la fiesta del pueblo!

2 Hay fiesta en el pueblo. ¿Qué actividades hay? Mira las fotos y lee.

3 Oscar dice qué actividades hay en las fiestas. Mira las fotos e indica el orden.

4 Escucha a Oscar. ¿Qué actividades le gustan? ¿Qué actividades no le gustan?

5 ¿Y tú? Habla con tu compañero(a).

Ejemplo Me gusta la verbena pero no me gustan las carreras.

1 **la verbena**

2 **las carreras**

3 **los cabezudos**

4 **los gigantes**

5 **las cucañas y los juegos para los chicos y las chicas**

6 **los fuegos artificiales**

7 **las canciones tradicionales**

8 **el baile tradicional**

9 **las carreras ciclistas**

10 **los churros**

11 **las ferias**

12 **el teatro infantil**

13 **la charanga**

6   **Mira el programa de fiestas.**

Hora	
1 A las *ocho de la mañana*	**Charanga** por las calles de la ciudad.
2	**Carrera Popular** en la Avenida San Sebastián; 10 kms.
3	**Ciclismo** en el Paseo de la Constitución.
4	**Gigantes y Cabezudos** en la Plaza del Pilar.
5	**Cucañas** en el parque grande.
6	**Teatro Infantil** en el Teatro Principal con la actuación del grupo 'Tres Tristes Tigres'.
7	**Baile Tradicional** en el Teatro Principal.
8	**Fuegos Artificiales** en la Plaza de San Francisco.
9	**Verbena** en el Paseo de la Independencia con la actuación del grupo Mecano.

¡no escribas aquí!

   **Escucha el programa de radio. Escribe las horas.**

B   **¿Adónde van?**

7   **Escucha y lee el ejemplo.**

Tessa ¿quieres ir a bailar a la verbena?

A las once.

Sí. ¿A qué hora es?

Vale. Hasta luego.

Invita a tu compañero(a) a la fiesta. Cambia.

8   **¿Qué son cucañas? Son juegos para los chicos y las chicas. Mira:**

¿Hay juegos similares en tu país? Habla con tu compañero(a).

9 **Lee la postal de Elena a Tessa.**

Querida Tessa:

¡Son las fiestas de
Zaragoza! ¡Son estupendas!
Hay muchas cosas
divertidas para todos.
Me gustan los cabezudos
y la verbena. Te mando un
programa y unas fotos.
En una foto llevo el traje
regional para la procesión.
Pero para el baile y las
cucañas llevo vaqueros.
Un abrazo,
Elena

 ¿Qué foto corresponde a cada frase? Escribe la frase y el número de la foto.

10 **Habla con tu compañero(a). ¿Tienes fiestas similares en tu pueblo o país? ¿Qué juegos hay?**

11 **Escribe una postal a Elena sobre las fiestas y juegos de *tu* país. Si quieres, ¡inventa!**

Aventura Semanal – ¿Sabes?

Las fiestas de Puerto Rico

Puerto Rico es el país de origen de la música salsa. Las maracas y el güiro son instrumentos típicos. En julio se celebra un brillante carnaval en Loiza, en la costa este, de origen africano. El traje tradicional de Puerto Rico es blanco y de muchos colores. Mira las fotos.

cantantes en traje regional
trajes de fiesta
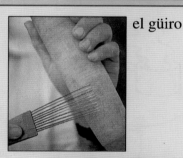
el güiro

las maracas

¡Ya sabes!

Vocabulario de la fiesta: la verbena, la charanga, los gigantes y los cabezudos, los fuegos artificiales, las cucañas, las ferias, las carreras, el teatro infantil, etc.

Autoevaluación En el campamento

1 **¿Qué haces todo los días por la mañana?**
Escribe 7 frases.

Ejemplo = Me despierto.

(14 puntos)

2 **Une los dibujos con las frases.**

(6 puntos)

1 Lavo la ropa.	4 Limpio mi cuarto.
2 Arreglo mis cosas.	5 Lavo los platos.
3 Preparo la comida.	6 Ordeno mis cosas.

3 **Escribe el horario de *tu* campamento.**
Incluye 10 actividades.

(30 puntos)

4 **¿Qué tiempo hace hoy?**
Ejemplo 1 = Hace fresco.

(14 puntos)

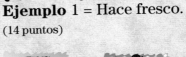

5 **Mira el cuerpo. Escribe 10 nombres.**

(20 puntos)

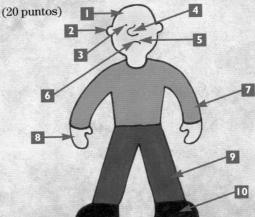

6 **¿Qué tal estás? Mira los**
dibujos y escribe frases.
Ejemplo 1 = Estoy enfermo.

(16 puntos)

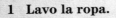
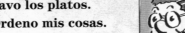

Total: /100

F

... y en broma

Un chiste ...

Gramática

Nombres — Nouns

These are words like **chico** (*boy*), **libro** (*book*), etc.

Masculino o femenino — Masculine or feminine

1 Nouns are either masculine or feminine. Nouns ending in **-o** are usually masculine. Nouns ending in **-a** are usually feminine.

For people:

chic**o**	*boy* (m)
chic**a**	*girl* (f)

and also for things:

lapicer**o**	*pencil* (m)
reg**la**	*ruler* (f)

There are a few exceptions to this rule and they have to be learnt as you go along:

dí**a**	*day* (m)
man**o**	*hand* (f)

2 If the masculine noun ends in a consonant (**-r, -l, -d**), add **-a** to form the feminine noun:

profesor	*teacher* (male)
profesor**a**	*teacher* (female)

3 Nouns ending in **-e** are the same in both masculine and feminine forms:

estudiante	*student* (male or female)
cantante	*singer* (male or female)

4 Many nouns do not show clearly from their endings whether they are masculine or feminine. These have to be learned as you go along. Here are some examples:

rotulador	*felt-tip pen* (m)
canción	*song* (f)
compás	*compasses* (m)

Plural — Plural

If we want to talk about *more than one* person or thing we use the plural.

1 Add **-s** if the noun ends in a vowel (**-o, -a,** or **-e**):

chico	chico**s**
chica	chica**s**
estudiante	estudiante**s**

2 Add **-es** if the noun ends in a consonant (eg **-r, -d, -l, -n**, etc.):

rotulador	rotulador**es**
actividad	actividad**es**

El artículo definido — The definite article

The definite article is used like *the* in English.

> el/los = *the (m)*
> la/las = *the (f)*

	Masculine	Feminine
Singular	**el** chico *the boy*	**la** chica *the girl*
Plural	**los** chicos *the boys*	**las** chicas *the girls*

The article can help you to learn whether a noun is masculine or feminine.

El artículo indefinido — The indefinite article

The indefinite article is used like *a* or *an* in the singular and *some* or *any* in the plural.

> un, una = *a/any*
> unos, unas = *some*

	Masculine	Feminine
Singular	**un** rotulador	**una** regla
Plural	**unos** rotuladores	**unas** reglas

Note: The plural masculine form is used if there are some male and some female members in the group.

un hermano	+ **un** hermano	= **unos** hermano**s**
una hermana	+ **una** hermana	= **unas** hermana**s**
un hermano	+ **una** hermana	= **unos** hermano**s**

Note: The indefinite articles are *not* used in the following cases:

1 Professions:

Soy estudiante.   *I'm a student.*

2 Questions and negations:

¿Tienes hermanos?
Do you have any brothers and sisters?
No tengo hermanos.
I don't have any brothers and sisters.

3 With **hay**:

¿Hay estudiantes?
Are there any students?
No, no hay estudiantes.
No, there aren't any students.

4 With plurals:

Quiero patatas.   *I want some potatoes.*

Adjetivos   Adjectives

Adjectives describe what something or someone is like. These are words like **bueno** (*good*), **simpático** (*nice*), etc.

1 Adjectives in Spanish usually appear immediately *after* the noun:

una chica **simpática**
a nice girl
el gato **pequeño**
the small cat

2 Adjectives *agree* with the noun. This means that if the noun is masculine, the adjective is also masculine. If the noun is feminine, the adjective is also feminine:

el chic**o** es simpátic**o**
the boy is nice (m)
la chic**a** es simpátic**a**
the girl is nice (f)

If the noun is in the plural, the adjective is also in the plural, and still agrees with the noun:

los chicos son simpátic**os**
the boys are nice (m)
las chicas son simpátic**as**
the girls are nice (f)

Note: Like nouns, adjectives ending in **-o** usually indicate masculine and those ending in **-a** usually indicate feminine.

el perr**o** fe**o**
the ugly dog (m)
la chic**a** alt**a**
the tall girl (f)

3 Adjectives *not* ending in **-o** *do not* change their form to agree with the noun. These are:

Adjectives ending in consonants (**-l**, **-n**, etc.):

un estuche **azul**
a blue pencil case (m)
una cartera **azul**
a blue school bag (f)
la mesa **marrón**
the brown table (m)
el abrigo **marrón**
the brown coat (f)

Adjectives ending in **e**:

un país **grande**
a big country (m)
una ciudad **grande**
a big city (f)

Adjectives of colour ending in **-a** do not change:

un rotulador naranj**a**
an orange felt-tip pen (m)
una goma naranj**a**
an orange rubber (f)
el coche ros**a**
the pink car (m)
la bicicleta ros**a**
the pink bicycle (f)

Note: Unlike the other adjectives in this section, nationalities which end in a consonant, *add* an **-a** to describe feminine things and people.

un chico español
a Spanish boy (m)
la chica español**a**
the Spanish girl (f)

Gramática

Adjetivos posesivos
Possessive adjectives

Possessive adjectives indicate *who* something belongs to.

Singular	mi *my*	tu *your*	su *his/her*
Plural	mis *my*	tus *your*	sus *his/her*

1 They appear *before* the noun.

2 They are different from English in that they can be singular or plural, depending on what they are describing, *not* the person who owns it.

mi libro	*my book* (sing)
mis libros	*my books* (plur)
tu libro	*your book* (sing)
tus libros	*your books* (plur)
su libro	*his/her books* (sing)
sus libros	*his/her books* (plur)

Note: If we talk about parts of the body we use **el** and **la** instead of the words for *my*, etc.

Me duele **la** cabeza.   ***My*** head aches.

Pronombres personales
Personal pronouns

There are different kinds of personal pronouns:

1 Those like *I, you, he/she* in English:

yo	*I*
tú/usted	*you/you (polite)*
él/ella	*he, it (m)/she, it (f)*
nosotros(as)	*we*
vosotros(as)/ustedes	*you/you (polite)*
ellos/ellas	*they (m/f)*

Note: In normal conversation **yo, tú, él/ella**, etc., are not used except for emphasis:

A ¿De dónde eres?
   Where are you from?
B Soy de Madrid.
   I am from Madrid.
A **Yo** soy de Barcelona.
   I am from Barcelona.

2 Pronouns that are similar to *me, you, him/her,* etc. These are called object pronouns.

me	*me*
te	*you*
le	*him/her/it*
nos	*us*
os	*you*
les	*them*

Me duele la cabeza.
My head aches.
(*Literally*: My head hurts me.)

Object pronouns (**me, te, le**, etc.) have to be used with certain verbs, such as **gustar**, etc.

Me gusta la playa.
I like the beach.
(*Literally*: The beach pleases me.)
¿Te gusta la playa?
Do you like the beach?
Le interesa la literatura.
He/She is interested in literature.
(*Literally*: Literature interests him/her.)

3 In Spanish there are special words for *with me* and *with you*:

conmigo	*with me*
contigo	*with you*

Conmigo and **contigo** are written as one word.

¿Quieres ir al cine **conmigo**?
Do you want to go to the cinema with me?
Quiero jugar al fútbol **contigo**.
I want to play football with you.

To say *with him* or *with us* etc. in Spanish we just use the normal object pronouns.

Quiero ir a la tienda **con él**.
I want to go to the shop with him.

Pronombres reflexivos
Reflexive pronouns

Reflexive pronouns occur with reflexive verbs. We use reflexive verbs when the action refers back to the person who does it, similar to verbs in English which use *myself, yourself,* etc.

me	*myself*
te	*yourself*
se	*himself/herself/itself*
nos	*ourselves*
os	*yourselves*
se	*themselves*

Here are some examples:

vestirse
Me visto.
I get dressed.
(*Literally*: I dress myself.)

levantarse
¿A qué hora **te** levantas?
What time do you get up?
Me levanto a las siete.
I get up at seven.
(*Literally*: I get myself up at seven.)

Note: **llamarse** has a similar construction:

¿Cómo te llamas?
What is your name?
(*Literally*: What do you call yourself?)

Adjetivos y pronombres demostrativos
Demonstrative pronouns and adjectives

These are the words *this* and *these* in English.

l We use them as an adjective straight in front of the noun with *no accent*:

	Masculine	Feminine	
Singular	este	esta	*this*
Plural	estos	estas	*these*

Here are some examples:

Este gato.	*This cat.* (m)
Esta calculadora.	*This calculator.* (f)
Estos estudiantes.	*These students.* (m)
Estas sillas.	*These chairs.* (f)

2 They can also be used on their own as a pronoun, and then they *do have an accent*:

	Masculine	Feminine	
Singular	éste	ésta	*this (one)*
Plural	éstos	éstas	*these (ones)*

Éste es mi padre.	*This is my father.*
Éstas son mis hermanas.	*These are my sisters.*
Quiero **éste**.	*I want this one.*

Note: There is also a neuter form **esto**, which *does not* have an accent:

Quiero esto.
I want this.

Números   Numbers

There are two types of numbers, *cardinal* numbers and *ordinal* numbers.

l Cardinal numbers are words like *one, two*, etc. They do not change form up to 199, except for the number *one*, which also has a feminine form.

Note: Numbers up to 29 are written as one word.

1	uno/una	21	veintiuno
2	dos	22	veintidós
3	tres	23	veintitrés
4	cuatro	24	veinticuatro
5	cinco	25	veinticinco
6	seis	26	veintiséis
7	siete	27	veintisiete
8	ocho	28	veintiocho
9	nueve	29	veintinueve
10	diez	30	treinta
11	once	31	treinta y uno
12	doce	32	treinta y dos
13	trece		(etc.)
14	catorce	40	cuarenta
15	quince	50	cincuenta
16	dieciséis	60	sesenta
17	diecisiete	70	setenta
18	dieciocho	80	ochenta
19	diecinueve	90	noventa
20	veinte		

Note: When placed before a masculine noun, **uno** changes to **un**:

Quiero **un** bolígrafo.   *I want a pen.*

Gramática

Numbers from 200 have a masculine and feminine form, depending on the noun they refer to.

100 cien
101 ciento uno (etc.)
200 doscientos(as)
300 trescientos(as)
400 cuatrocientos(as)
500 quinientos(as)
600 seiscientos(as)
700 setecientos(as)
800 ochocientos(as)
900 novecientos(as)
1000 mil
2000 dos mil (etc.)

Here are some examples:

En mi colegio hay doscientos chicos.
In my school there are two hundred boys.
En mi colegio hay quinientas chicas.
In my school there are five hundred girls.
Trescientos dólares.
Three hundred dollars.
Trescientas pesetas.
Three hundred pesetas.

Dates in Spanish appear as cardinal numbers with the definite article, **el**.

El **2** de octubre.
The 2nd of October.

2 Ordinal numbers are words like *first, second, third*, etc.
All ordinal numbers have a masculine and a feminine form. Unlike most adjectives, they normally appear *before* the noun:

el **segundo** piso
the second floor
la **segunda** casa
the second house

Note: **primero** (*first*) and **tercero** (*third*) drop the **-o** before a masculine noun:

primer piso   *first floor*
tercer año   *third year*

La hora — Time

To talk about the time in Spanish you have to use the verb **ser**:

Es la una.
It's one o'clock.
Son las dos.
It's two o'clock.
Son las dos y media.
It's half past two.

Here are some useful phrases:

¿Que hora es?
What time is it?
¿A qué hora tienes matemáticas?
What time do you have maths?
A las nueve.
At nine o'clock.
De nueve a diez.
From nine to ten.

Preguntas — Questions

In Spanish all questions have two question marks, an upside-down one at the beginning of the question, ¿, and a normal one at the end, **?**.

¿Cómo te llamas?   *What's your name?*

The intonation of a question is important and questions are usually spoken with a rise in intonation on the last syllables of the phrase. There are two ways to ask questions:

1 Add the question marks to a normal affirmative sentence:

¿Javier es de México?
Is Javier from Mexico?

2 Put the verb in front of the subject of the question:

¿Es Javier de México?
Is Javier from Mexico?

Interrogativos — Question words

Question words are used to start questions. Examples of question words in English are *what?*, *how?*. Question words *always* have accents.

¿Qué ...? — *What ...?*

¿Qué quieres?
What do you want?

¿Dónde ...? — *Where ...?*

¿De dónde eres?
Where are you from?

¿Adónde ...? — *Where (to) ...?*

¿Adónde vas?
Where are you going?

¿Cuándo ...? — *When ...?*

¿Cuándo es tu cumpleaños?
When is your birthday?

¿Cuánto(a)/ cuántos(as) ...? — *How much/many ...?*

¿Cuánto es?
How much is it?

¿Cuánta leche quieres?
How much milk do you want?

¿Cuántos años tienes?
How old are you?

¿Cuántas hermanas tienes?
How many sisters have you got?

¿Cómo ...? — *What ...?*

¿Cómo es?
What's it like?

¿Cómo te llamas?
What's your name?

Preposiciones — Prepositions

Here are the most common prepositions you will see:

a	*at, to*
con	*with*
de	*about, from, of*
desde	*from, since*
en	*in, on, at*
entre	*between*
hacia	*towards*
hasta	*until*
para	*for, in order to*
por	*for*
sin	*without*

Here are some examples of how the most important prepositions are used:

a — ***at, to***
This word is used in a number of different ways:

1 In time expressions:

Tengo matemáticas **a** las diez.
*I have maths **at** ten.*

2 To indicate direction:

Voy **a** la playa.
*I'm going **to** the beach.*

3 Before a person:

Invito **a** María al cine.
I invite María to the cinema.

4 With the verb **ir** + **a** + infinitive to talk about what you are about to do:

Voy **a** jugar con mis amigos.
I'm going to play with my friends.

con — ***with***
Voy a la piscina **con** mis amigos.
I go to the pool with my friends.

Gramática

de   *from, of*

This word can also be used in a number of ways:

1 To describe where someone or something is from:

> Soy **de** Barcelona.
> *I am from Barcelona.*

2 To show who something belongs to:

> La casa **de** Isabel.
> *Isabel's house.*

3 To describe what something is about:

> Es una película **de** aventuras.
> *It's an adventure film.*

4 To describe what something is for:

> El saco **de** dormir.
> *The sleeping bag.*
> (*Literally:* a bag for sleeping)

desde   *from*

> Hay 600 kms **desde** Madrid a Barcelona.
> *It's 600 kms from Madrid to Barcelona.*

en   *in, on, at*

> Estoy **en** la playa.
> *I'm at/on the beach.*
> El jersey está **en** el armario.
> *The sweater is in the wardrobe.*

entre   *between*

> Zaragoza está **entre** Barcelona y Madrid.
> *Zaragoza is between Barcelona and Madrid.*

Preposiciones y expresiones de lugar
Prepositions and expressions of place

These words are used with the verb **estar** to express where somebody or something is. They add **de** if they are followed by a noun.

cerca (de)   *near (to)*

> Barcelona está **cerca de** la playa.
> *Barcelona is near the beach.*
> Madrid está **cerca**.
> *Madrid is nearby.*

lejos (de)   *far (from)*

> Barcelona está **lejos de** Madrid.
> *Barcelona is a long way from Madrid.*

delante (de)   *in front (of)*

> El coche está **delante de** la casa.
> *The car is in front of the house.*

detrás (de)   *behind*

> El parque está **detrás de** la casa.
> *The park is behind the house.*

al lado (de)   *next to*

> El salón está **al lado del** comedor.
> *The living room is next to the dining room.*

enfrente (de)   *opposite*

> El baño está **enfrente de** la cocina.
> *The bathroom is opposite the kitchen.*

debajo (de)   *under, underneath, below*

> El libro está **debajo de** la cama.
> *The book is underneath the bed.*

encima (de)   *on, on top of, above*

> El gato está **encima de** la cama.
> *The cat is on the bed.*

Direcciones   Directions

a la izquierda
on/to the left

a la derecha
on/to the right

todo recto
straight on

al final (de)
at the end (of)

al fondo (de)
at the end, at the bottom (of)

> La calle Molina es la primera **a la izquierda**.
> *Calle Molina is the first on the left.*

> La iglesia está en la segunda calle **a la derecha**.
> *The church is in the second street on the right.*

> El hospital está **todo recto**, **al final de** esta calle.
> *The hospital is straight on, at the end of this street.*

> La cocina está **al fondo**.
> *The kitchen is right at the end.*

Contracciones — Contractions

A contraction is where two words join together. There are only two cases in Spanish:

1   **a + el = al**   *to the*

Voy **al** cine.
I'm going to the cinema.

2   **de + el = del**   *of the*

El libro **del** profesor.
The teacher's book.

Note: **a + la(s)/los** and **de + la(s)/los** do not contract:

Voy **a la** piscina.
I'm going to the pool.
El libro **de los** profesores.
The teachers' book.

Conjunciones — Conjunctions

Conjunctions are words used to link two words together, like *and* in English.

y = *and*

El chico **y** la chica.
The boy and the girl.

Estudio matemáticas **y** ciencias.
I study maths and science.

Note: Before Spanish words beginning with **i-** and **hi-** we use **e** instead of **y**.

Escucha **e** indica.
Listen and indicate.

Expresiones de tiempo — Expressions of time

We use time expressions to describe when we do something or when something happens.

mañana   *tomorrow*
Voy a la piscina **mañana**.
I'm going to the pool tomorrow.

todos los días   *every day*
Todos los días voy al colegio.
I go to school every day.

por la mañana   *in the morning*
Estudio **por la mañana**.
I study in the morning.

por la tarde   *in the afternoon*
Juego con mis amigos **por la tarde**.
I play with my friends in the afternoon.

el fin de semana   *at the weekend*
Voy a la playa **el fin de semana**.
I go to the beach at the weekend.

el domingo/los domingos *on Sunday/s*
Los domingos visito a mis abuelos.
On Sunday I visit my grandparents.

Adverbios — Adverbs

There are different kinds of adverbs. The most common and useful ones are the following:

1 These express how you feel.

bien	*well*
mal	*ill*
regular	*so-so, all right*

Estoy **bien**.	*I'm well.*
¿Estás **mal**?	*Are you ill?*
¿Qué tal estás?	*How are you?*
Regular.	*So-so.*

2 To say *yes* and *no*:

| Sí | *Yes* |
| No | *No* |

Note: To make a sentence into a negative simply place the word **no** at the beginning of an affirmative sentence:

Quiero té.
I want some tea.
No quiero té.
*I **don't** want any tea.*

3 Words that mean *a lot, very*, etc.

Come **mucho.**
He eats a lot.
La casa es **muy** grande.
The house is very big.

Gramática

Verbos Verbs

Verbs are words like **hablar** (*to speak*), **comer** (*to eat*) and **vivir** (*to live*).

Verbs show when something is done and who is involved. There are three parts to a verb, called *tense*, *person* and *verb endings*.

1 Tense
The tense of a verb shows *when* something is done, eg past, present, future.

2 Person
The person of a verb indicates *who* is doing the main action of the verb. The person can be either singular or plural.

yo	*I*
tú	*you*
él/ella	*he/she*
usted	*you (polite)*
nosotros(as)	*we*
vosotros(as)	*you*
ellos(as)	*they*
ustedes	*you (polite)*

Note: These words are not often used as the person is indicated by the different verb endings.

3 Verb endings
Verb endings show *who* is performing the action of the verb.

> Cen**o** a las ocho.
> *I eat supper at eight.*
> ¿Tien**es** un bolígrafo?
> *Do **you** have a pen?*

Types of verbs

In the dictionary you will find the infinitive form of the verb. In English, the infinitive has the word *to* before it, eg *to eat*. In Spanish the infinitive is indicated by **-ar, -er,** or **-ir** at the end of the verb. The main part of the verb is called the stem.

There are three types of verbs:
>   those ending in **-ar** (like **cenar**),
>   those ending in **-er** (like **comer**), and
>   those ending in **-ir** (like **vivir**).

Regular verbs

Cenar, **comer** and **vivir** are *regular* verbs and they follow an easy-to-learn pattern. Others are *irregular* and have to be learnt as you go along.

When talking about the present, regular verb types have the following endings:

-ar: cenar   *to have dinner/supper*

(yo)	cen**o**
(tú)	cen**as**
(él/ella/usted)	cen**a**
(nosotros(as))	cen**amos**
(vosotros(as))	cen**áis**
(ellos/ellas/ustedes)	cen**an**

Other regular **-ar** verbs include:

desayunar	*to have breakfast*
bailar	*to dance*
llevar	*to carry, wear*

-er: comer   *to eat*

(yo)	com**o**
(tú)	com**es**
(él/ella/usted)	com**e**
(nosotros(as))	com**emos**
(vosotros(as))	com**éis**
(ellos/ellas/ustedes)	com**en**

Other regular **-er** verbs include:

leer	*to read*
beber	*to drink*

-ir: vivir   *to live*

(yo)	viv**o**
(tú)	viv**es**
(él/ella/usted)	viv**e**
(nosotros(as))	viv**imos**
(vosotros(as))	viv**ís**
(ellos/ellas/ustedes)	viv**en**

Other regular **-ir** verbs include:

describir	*to describe*
unir	*to link, to join*
escribir	*to write*

All *regular* verbs will follow this common pattern. Notice the similarities and differences between the three verb types:

-ar	-er	-ir
cen-**o**	com-**o**	escrib-**o**
cen-**as**	com-**es**	escrib-**es**
cen-**a**	com-**e**	escrib-**e**
cen-**amos**	com-**emos**	escrib-**imos**
cen-**áis**	com-**éis**	escrib-**ís**
cen-**an**	com-**en**	escrib-**en**

Note: To form the negative we again simply put **no** immediately before the verb:

No como carne.   *I don't eat meat.*

Irregular verbs

Spanish has irregular verbs and these have to be learnt as you go along, although again there are some patterns.

Verbs can be irregular in different ways. Here are some examples:

1 Verbs where *one letter* in the stem changes, except in the **we** and **you** plural forms:

e = ie
querer *to want*

quiero
quieres
quiere
queremos
queréis
quieren

Other verbs which follow this pattern include:

cerrar   *to close*
comenzar   *to begin*

o = ue
dormir *to sleep*

duermo
duermes
duerme
dormimos
dormís
duermen

Other verbs which follow this pattern include:

doler   *to hurt*
llover   *to rain*
poder   *to be able to*

u = ue
jugar *to play*

juego
juegas
juega
jugamos
jugáis
juegan

Note: The above verbs are all in the regular form in the 1st and 2nd person plural.

2 In some verbs one letter in the first part of the word is changed to **g**, but only when talking about *I* in the present tense.

hacer *to do, to make*
hago   *I do/make*

salir *to leave, to go out*
salgo   *I leave*

3 In some verbs one letter in the stem changes *and* also one letter is changed to **g**:

tener *to have*

tengo
tienes
tiene
tenemos
tenéis
tienen

4 Some verbs add **y** in the first person:

estar *to be*	estoy	*I am*
ser *to be*	soy	*I am*
dar *to give*	doy	*I give*

5 A few verbs are irregular in all persons:

ir *to go*

voy
vas
va
vamos
vais
van

Gramática

6 Whereas English has only one verb for *to be*, Spanish has two: **ser** and **estar**.

Ser	Estar	
soy	estoy	*I am*
eres	estás	*you are*
es	está	*he/she/it is*
somos	estamos	*we are*
sois	estáis	*you are*
son	están	*they are*

Ser

We use **ser** to talk about permanent features of people, animals or things:

1 Nationality:

Soy español.
I'm Spanish.

2 Appearance:

Eres alto.
You are tall.

3 Personality:

Es aburrido.
He is boring.

4 Characteristics:

Es grande.
It's big.

5 Qualities, eg of a book, film, etc.:

Es interesante.
It's interesting.

Estar

We use **estar** to talk about:

1 Where someone is:

Estoy en la playa.
I am on the beach.

2 Where something or a place is:

Madrid **está** en el centro de España.
Madrid is in the centre of Spain.

3 How someone feels (about something):

Estoy aburrido(a).
I am bored.
Está enferma.
She is ill.
Está cansado.
He is tired.

Two verbs together

The verb **querer** can be used with other verbs:

querer + infinitive   *to want to do something*

¿Quieres ir al cine?
Do you want to go to the cinema?
¿Quieres jugar?
Do you want to play?
No quiero ver esta película.
I don't want to see this film.

See also **gustar** on the next page.

Other verb constructions

Some verbs are used with other words to produce a new meaning.

1 The verb **hacer** is used in the following expressions to describe the weather:

Hace frío.
It's cold.
Hace calor.
It's hot.

2 The verb **tener** has many different uses in Spanish and can be used to express the following meanings:

Age:

Tengo doce años.
I am twelve years old.

Possession:

Tengo un bolígrafo.
I have a pen.
La casa **tiene** seis habitaciones.
The house has six rooms.

3 The verb **gustar** is used for the equivalent of the English *to like*, but the form is roughly translated as *to please*.
Remember that object pronouns (**me, te, le,** etc.) must be used with **gustar**.

Me gusta el chocolate.
I like chocolate.
(*Literally*: Chocolate pleases me.)

When we want to say that we like two or more things we use **gustan**.

Me gustan las películas románticas.
I like romantic films.

The negative is formed by placing **no** before the object pronoun.

No me gusta el teatro.
I don't like the theatre
No me gustan las salchichas.
I don't like sausages.

We use **le** to talk about what *another* person likes:

Le gusta el fútbol.
He/She likes football
No le gusta el baloncesto.
He/She doesn't like basketball.
Le gustan los animales.
He/She likes animals.
No le gustan las salchichas.
He/She doesn't like sausages.

The verb **gustar** can also be followed by an infinitive to form the equivalent of *I like doing*:

Me gusta bailar.
I like dancing.

4 Other verbs which use the object pronoun in a similar way are:

doler *to hurt*

Me duele la cabeza.
My head aches.
(*Literally*: My head hurts me.)
Me duelen los pies.
My feet hurt.
(*Literally*: My feet hurt me).

interesar *to be interested in*

Me interesa la literature.
Literature interests me.
Me interesan las novelas
Novels interest me.
¿Te interesa el cine?
Are you interested in the cinema?
No **le interesa** la música.
He/She isn't interested in music.

Hay — There is/are

The word **hay** is used for the equivalent of *there is* and *there are* in English, and does not change.

Hay un laboratorio.
There is a laboratory.
Hay estudiantes.
There are students.
No hay agua.
There isn't any water.

Note: There is no article before the noun in the plural or for negatives.

A

a *at; to*
el abrazo *hug*
un abrazo *love from (letter)*
un abrazo fuerte *lots of love (letter)*
el abrigo *overcoat*
abril *April*
abrir *to open*
la abuela *grandmother*
la abuelita *grandma, granny*
el abuelito *grandad, grandpa*
el abuelo *grandfather*
aburrido(a) *bored*
el accidente *accident*
aceptar *to accept*
acostarse *to go to bed*
la actividad *activity*
adiós *goodbye*
adivinar *to guess*
¿adónde? *where (to)?*
adoptar *to adopt*
la agenda *diary, notebook*
agosto *August*
el agua (f) *water*
el agua mineral (f) *mineral water*
el águila (f) *eagle*
ahora *now*
el abeto *fir tree*
el alemán *German language*
alemán/alemana *German*
Alemania *Germany*
la alfombra *carpet*
alto(a) *high, tall*
amarillo(a) *yellow*
el amigo/la amiga *friend*
los dibujos animados *cartoons*
el animal *animal*
el anorak *anorak*
el anuncio *advertisement*
el año *year*
el apartamento *apartment*
aproximadamente *approximately*
aquí *here*
aprender *to learn*
el/la árabe *Arab*
árabe *Arabic*
el árbol *tree*
Argentina *Argentina*
argentino(a) *Argentinian*
el armario *wardrobe, cupboard*
el arquitecto/la arquitecta *architect*
la arquitectura *architecture*
arreglar *to tidy up*
el arte *art*
así *in this way*
el taller de arte *art room*
el artículo *article*
la asignatura *school subject*

la atención *attention*
el atletismo *athletics*
atrás *backwards, behind*
auténtico(a) *authentic*
el autobús *bus*
la autoevaluación *self-evaluation*
el automóvil *automobile*
la avenida *avenue*
la aventura *adventure*
el aventurero/la aventurera *adventurer*
ayudar *to help*
azul *blue*

B

el bádminton *badminton*
bailar *to dance*
el baile *dancing*
bajar *to go down, descend*
el bajo *bass (musical instrument)*
bajo(a) *short*
la planta baja *ground floor*
el baloncesto *basketball*
el balonmano *handball*
el banco *bank*
la bandera *flag*
el bañador *swimming costume/trunks*
bañarse *to have a bath, bathe*
el baño *bath*
el cuarto de baño *bathroom*
la base de datos *database*
los bastos *clubs (cards)*
la batería *drums*
el batido *milkshake*
el bebé (m/f) *baby*
beber *to drink*
la bebida *drink*
el béisbol *baseball*
bengalí *Bengali*
la biblioteca *library*
la bicicleta *bicycle*
el bidé *bidet*
bien *good; well*
el bigote *moustache*
tener bigote *to have a moustache*
bilingüe *bilingual*
el billete *note (money); ticket (transport)*
la biología *biology*
blanco(a) *white*
la blusa *blouse*
la boca *mouth*
el bocadillo *sandwich (with crusty bread)*
el bolígrafo *ballpoint pen*
Bolivia *Bolivia*
la bolsa *bag*
la bolsa de aseo *toilet bag*
bonito(a) *pretty*
Bosnia *Bosnia*
bosnio(a) *Bosnian*
el bosque *wood (with trees)*

la bota *boot*
el boxeo *boxing*
la braga *knickers*
el brazo *arm*
la broma *joke*
en broma *in fun*
el bronceador *suntan lotion*
la bruja *witch*
el bucardo *goat*
bueno *good, OK*
buenas noches *good night*
buenas tardes *good afternoon, good evening*
buenos días *good day, good morning*
el buitre *vulture*
la bufanda *scarf*
el burro *donkey*
buscar *to look for*

C

el caballo *horse*
la cabeza *head*
el cabezudo *festival figure with big head*
cada *each, every*
el café *coffee*
la cafetería *café*
el calcetín *sock*
la calculadora *calculator*
el calendario *calendar*
la calle *street*
el calor *heat*
hace calor *it's hot*
los calzonzillos *underpants*
la cama *bed*
cambiar *to change, exchange*
la camisa *shirt*
la camiseta *T-shirt; vest*
el campamento *campsite; summer camp*
el campeón/la campeona *champion*
la tienda de camping *tent*
el campo *countryside; field*
las islas Canarias *Canary Islands*
la canción *song*
cansado(a) *tired*
el/la cantante *singer (m/f)*
cantar *to sing*
la cantimplora *flask*
el carnaval *carnival*
la carne *meat*
la carrera *race*
la carta *letter*
las cartas *playing cards*
la cartera *school bag*
la casa *house; home*
en casa *at home*
cascabelero(a) *scatterbrained*
la casilla *box*
el cassette *cassette*
el castellano *Castilian, Spanish (language)*
castellano(a) *Castilian*

Castilla *Castile*
el catalán *Catalan language*
catalán *Catalan (adj)*
Cataluña *Catalonia*
catorce *fourteen*
celebrar *to celebrate*
celebrarse *to be celebrated*
la cena *dinner; supper*
cenar *to have dinner/supper*
el centro *centre*
el centro de la ciudad *town centre*
el centro cultural *cultural centre*
el cepillo de dientes *toothbrush*
la cerámica *ceramics, pottery*
cerca (de) *near (to)*
el cerdo *pig; pork*
los cereales *cereals*
cero *zero*
cerrar *to close*
el ciclismo *cycling*
cien *hundred*
ciento *one hundred*
la ciencia ficción *science fiction*
las ciencias *sciences*
las ciencias naturales *natural sciences*
las ciencias sociales *social sciences*
cinco *five*
cincuenta *fifty*
el cine *cinema*
la cinta *tape*
la ciudad *city; large town*
la clase *class; classroom; type*
la clínica *clinic*
el club *social club*
el coche *car*
la cocina *kitchen; cooker*
el codo *elbow*
el colegio *school*
Colombia *Columbia*
colombiano(a) *Columbian*
el color *colour*
el comedor *dining room*
comer *to eat*
la comida *food; meal*
como *like, similar to*
¿cómo? *how? what?*
¿cómo es? *what's it like?*
¿cómo se escribe? *how do you spell it?*
¿cómo te llamas? *what's your name?*
la cómoda *chest of drawers*
cómodo(a) *comfortable*
el compañero/la compañera *companion; classmate*
comparar *to compare*
el compás *compasses*
la competición *competition*
completar *to complete*
comprar *to buy*
comprobar *to check, compare*
con *with*

el concierto *concert*
el conejo *rabbit*
el congelador *freezer*
conmigo *with me*
la constitución *constitution*
contento(a) *happy*
contestar *to answer*
contigo *with you*
continuar *to continue*
la concha *shell*
la copa *glass (for drinking)*
el corazón *heart*
correcto(a) *correct*
corregir *to correct*
la cortina *curtain*
la cosa *thing*
la costa *coast*
Costa Rica *Costa Rica*
el crucigrama (m) *crossword*
cruzar *to cross*
el cuaderno *exercise book*
el cuadro *grid, chart; picture*
de cuadros *check pattern*
¿cuál? *which?*
cuando *when*
¿cuándo? *when?*
¿cuánto? *how much?*
¿cuánto es? *how much is it?*
¿cuántos(as)? *how many?*
cuarenta *forty*
el cuarto *room; quarter*
el cuarto de baño *bathroom*
el cuarto de libra *quarterpounder (hamburger)*
cuatro *four*
cuatrocientos(as) *four hundred*
Cuba *Cuba*
cubano(a) *Cuban*
la cucaña *festival game*
el cuerpo *body*
cultural *cultural*
el centro cultural *cultural centre*
el cumpleaños *birthday*
cumpleaños feliz *happy birthday*
el curso *course*

CH

el champú *shampoo*
el chándal *track suit*
la chaqueta *jacket*
el chico/la chica *boy/girl*
Chile *Chile*
la chimenea *chimney*
China *China*
chino(a) *Chinese*
el chino *Chinese language*
la chispa *spark*
el chiste *joke*
el chocolate *chocolate (food/drink)*

la chova *crow*
el churro *sweet fritter*

D

el dado *dice (for game)*
la danza *dance*
los datos *data*
la base de datos *database*
de *about; from; of*
debajo (de) *below; underneath*
los deberes *homework*
decir *to say, tell*
delante (de) *in front (of)*
el delfín *dolphin*
delgado(a) *slim, thin*
los demás *the others, the rest*
el dependiente/la dependienta *shop assistant*
el deporte *sport*
la derecha *right (direction)*
a la derecha *on/to the right*
desayunar *to have breakfast*
el desayuno *breakfast*
descansar *to relax, rest*
describir *to describe*
la descripción *description*
desde *from; since*
desear *to desire, wish for*
el desfile *street procession*
despacio *slow(ly)*
despertarse *to wake up*
después *afterwards; then*
la destreza *skill*
detrás (de) *behind*
el día *day*
todos los días *every day*
el diálogo *dialogue*
diario(a) *daily*
dibujar *to draw*
el dibujo *art (subject); drawing, picture*
los dibujos animados *cartoons*
el diccionario *dictionary*
diciembre *December*
dictar *to dictate*
diecinueve *nineteen*
dieciocho *eighteen*
dieciséis *sixteen*
diecisiete *seventeen*
el diente *tooth*
lavarse los dientes *brush one's teeth*
diez *ten*
la diferencia *difference*
diferente *different*
el dinero *money*
la dirección *address*
el director/la directora *director*
la discoteca *disco*
diseñar *to design*
el disfraz *disguise, fancy dress*

el disgusto *dislike*
divertido(a) *enjoyable, fun*
doce *twelve*
el dólar *dollar*
el dolor *hurt, pain*
doler *to hurt*
me duele el brazo *my arm hurts*
el dolor de cabeza *headache*
el domingo *Sunday*
donde *where*
¿dónde? *where?*
dormir *to sleep*
el saco de dormir *sleeping bag*
el dormitorio *bedroom*
dos *two*
doscientos(as) *two hundred*
el drama *drama*
durante *for (time)*
durar *to last*
la ducha *shower*
ducharse *to shower*

E

e *and (before i and hi only)*
Ecuador *Ecuador*
la edad *age*
el edelweiss *edelweiss*
el edificio *building*
la educación *education*
la educación física *physical education*
el ejemplo *example*
el ejercicio *exercise*
el *the (m)*
él *he, it (m)*
ella *she, it (f)*
ellos/ellas *they (m/f)*
elegir *to choose*
empezar *to begin, start*
en *in; on; at*
en punto *on time, exactly*
en total *altogether, in total*
encima (de) *on top (of)*
encontrar *to find*
la encuesta *survey*
enero *January*
enfadado(a) *angry*
enfermo(a) *ill*
enfrente (de) *opposite*
enorme *enormous*
la ensalada *salad*
la entrada *entrance; hallway; entrance ticket*
entrar *to enter*
entre *amongst; between*
la entrevista *interview*
enviar *to send*
el equipo *equipment; team*
equivalente *equivalent*
el error *mistake*

escalar *to climb, go up*
la escalera *stairs*
escocés/escocesa *Scottish (m/f)*
Escocia *Scotland*
escribir *to write*
¿cómo se escribe? *how is it spelt?*
la escuela *school*
escuchar *to listen*
escuchar música *to listen to music*
el espacio *space*
la espada *sword*
los espaguetis *spaghetti*
España *Spain*
el español *Spanish language*
español/española *Spanish (m/f)*
el espejo *mirror*
esperar *to wait*
el esqueleto *skeleton*
el esquí *skiing*
esquiar *to ski*
la estación *station; season*
el estadio *stadium*
el estadio de fútbol *football stadium*
los Estados Unidos *United States*
estadounidense *American (m/f)*
la estantería *shelf*
estar *to be (location/state)*
la estatura *height*
el este *east*
éste/ésta/esto *this (m/f)*
la esterilla *sunmat*
estos(as) *these*
el estuche *pencil case*
el/la estudiante *student (m/f)*
estudiar *to study*
estupendo(a) *great, wonderful*
Euskadi *Basque country*
el euskera *Basque language*
excelente *excellent*
la excursión *trip, excursion*
ir de excursión *to go on a trip*
explicar *explain*
la exposición *exhibition*
la expresión *expression*
el extranjero/la extranjera *foreigner*
el extranjero *abroad, overseas*
extranjero(a) *foreign*

F

la fábrica *factory*
la falda *skirt*
faltar *to be missing, lack*
la familia *family*
familiar *family (adj)*
famoso(a) *famous*
fantástico(a) *fantastic*
la farmacia *chemist shop*
favorito(a) *favourite*

febrero *february*
la fecha *date*
feliz *happy*
feliz cumpleaños *happy birthday*
feo(a) *ugly*
la feria *funfair*
la fiesta *festival; party*
el filete *fillet*
las Filipinas *Philippines*
el fin *end (film)*
el fin de semana *weekend*
el final *end (event)*
al final (de) *at the end (of)*
la ficha *form, card*
la flor *flower*
el fondo *bottom*
al fondo (de) *at the bottom (of)*
la foto (f) *photograph*
la fotografía *photography*
el francés *French language*
francés/francesa *French*
Francia *France*
la frase *sentence*
el fregadero *sink*
la fresa *strawberry*
fresco(a) *cool*
hace fresco *it's cool*
el frigo *fridge*
frío(a) *cold*
hace frío *it's cold*
la fruta *fruit*
los fuegos artificiales *fireworks*
la fuente *fountain; source*
fuerte *strong*
el fútbol *football*
el estadio de fútbol *football stadium*
el futbolín *table football*

G

las gafas *spectacles*
tener gafas *to wear glasses*
Gales *Wales*
galés/galesa *Welsh (m/f)*
Galicia *Galicia*
el gallego *Galician language*
gallego(a) *Galician*
la galleta *biscuit*
ganar *earn, win*
la garganta *throat*
la gaseosa *lemonade*
el gato *cat*
la gente *people*
la geografía *geography*
el gigante *giant*
la gimnasia *exercise, gymnastics*
el gimnasio *gymnasium*
la goma *eraser; rubber*
gordo(a) *fat*
la gorra *cap, hat*

el gorro *hat*
la gota *drop (of liquid)*
gracias *thank you*
el grado *degree (temperature)*
grande *big*
Grecia *Greece*
el griego *Greek language*
griego(a) *Greek*
gris *grey*
el grupo *group*
guapo(a) *beautiful*
Guatemala *Guatemala*
la guerra *war*
la película de guerra *war film*
de guerra *war (adj)*
Guinea Ecuatorial *Ecuatorial Guinea*
el güiro *musical instrument made of a gourd*
la guitarra *guitar*
gustar *to please, like*
me gusta la leche *I like milk*
el gusto *like*

H

la habitación *room*
hablar *to speak, talk*
hacer *to do, make*
hacia *towards*
la hamburguesa *hamburger*
hasta *until*
hasta luego *see you soon/later*
hay *there is/are*
el haya (f) *beech tree*
el helado *ice cream*
el hermano/la hermana *brother/sister*
los hermanos *brothers (and sisters)*
la historia *history; story*
el hockey *hockey*
el hockey patines *roller hockey*
hola *hello*
Honduras *Honduras*
la hora *hour; time*
¿qué hora es? *what time is it?*
el horario *timetable*
el hospital *hospital*
el hotel *hotel*
hoy *today*

I

ideal *ideal*
el idioma *language*
igual *identical*
imaginar *to imagine*
importante *important*
incluir *to include*
indicar *to indicate*
individualmente *individually*
infantil *for children*
la información *information*
la informática *information technology*

Inglaterra *England*
el inglés *English language*
inglés/inglesa *English*
la instrucción *instruction*
el intercambio *exchange*
interesante *interesting*
inventar *to invent*
el invierno *winter*
la invitación *invitation*
invitar a *to invite someone*
ir *to go*
ir de excursión *to go on a trip*
ir de vacaciones *to go on holiday*
Irlanda *Ireland*
irlandés/irlandesa *Irish*
la isla *island*
las islas Canarias *Canary Islands*
Italia *Italy*
el italiano *Italian language*
italiano(a) *Italian*
la izquierda *left*
a la izquierda *on/to the left*

J

el jabón *soap*
Jamaica *Jamaica*
jamaicano(a) *Jamaican*
el jardín *garden*
el jersey *jumper, sweater*
el judo *judo*
el juego *game*
la sala de juegos *games room*
el jueves *Thursday*
jugar *play (game)*
el juguete *toy*
julio *July*
junio *June*
juvenil *for young people*

L

la *the (f, sing)*
el laboratorio *laboratory*
el lado *side*
al lado (de) *beside, next to*
la lámpara *lamp*
el lapicero *pencil*
largo(a) *long*
las *the (f, plu)*
Latinoamérica *Latin America*
latinoamericano(a) *Latin American*
el lavabo *sink*
la lavandería *laundry*
lavar *to wash*
lavarse *to wash oneself*
lavarse los dientes *to clean one's teeth*
leer *to read*
lejos (de) *far (from)*
la lengua *language; tongue*
el lenguaje *language*

la letra *letter of the alphabet*
la sopa de letras *word-search game*
levantarse *to get up*
la leche *milk*
la libra esterlina *pound sterling*
la librería *bookshop*
el libro *book*
el limón *lemon*
limpiar *to clean*
la linterna *torch*
la lista *list*
la literatura *literature*
llamarse *to be called*
llegar *to arrive*
llevar *to carry, wear*
llover *to rain*
llueve *it's raining*
la lógica *logic*
la lotería *lottery*
luego *later, soon*
hasta luego *see you later/soon*
el lugar *place*
la luna *moon*
el lunes *Monday*

M

la madre *mother*
la magdalena *Spanish cupcake*
mal *unhappy, unwell*
la mamá *Mum*
mandar *to send*
la manera *manner*
la mano *(f) hand*
manual *manual*
los trabajos manuales *handicrafts*
la manualidad *manual craft/work*
el taller de manualidades *crafts workshop*
la manzana *apple*
la mañana *morning*
de/por la mañana *in the morning*
mañana *tomorrow*
el mapa *(m) map*
el maquillaje *make-up*
el/la mar *sea (m/f)*
las maracas *maracas*
la marca *brand, make*
marcar *to indicate, mark*
marrón *brown*
el martes *Tuesday*
marzo *March*
más *more; most*
las matemáticas *mathematics*
mayo *May*
mayor *older*
las medias *tights*
el médico/la médica *doctor*
mejor *best*
el mejor amigo *best friend*
la memoria *memory*

menor *younger*
el menú *menu*
merendar *to have an afternoon snack*
la merienda *afternoon snack*
el mes *month*
la mesa *table*
la mesilla *bedside table*
el metal *metal*
de metal *metal (adj)*
el metro *metre*
mexicano(a) *Mexican*
México *Mexico*
mi(s) *my*
el miércoles *Wednesday*
mil *thousand; one thousand*
mimar *to mime*
el agua mineral *(f) mineral water*
el minuto *minute*
mirar *to look at*
la mochila *rucksack*
moderno(a) *modern*
el monasterio *convent, monastery*
la moneda *coin*
el monitor/la monitora *monitor, supervisor*
el mono *monkey*
el monopatín *skateboard*
el monstruo *monster*
la montaña *mountain*
el monumento *monument*
la moqueta *fitted carpet*
moreno(a) *dark (hair, skin)*
los muebles *furniture*
mundial *world (adj)*
el mundo *world*
el museo *museum*
la música *music*
escuchar música *to listen to music*

N

nacional *national*
la nacionalidad *nationality*
nadar *to swim*
naranja *(adj) orange*
la naranja *orange*
el zumo de naranja *orange juice*
la nariz *nose*
la natación *swimming*
necesario(a) *necessary*
necesitar *to need*
negro(a) *black*
nevar *to snow*
Nicaragua *Nicaragua*
nieva *it's snowing*
ni ... no ... *neither ... nor ...*
la nieve *snow*
el niño/la niña *young boy/girl*
no *no; not*
la noche *night*
buenas noches *good evening, good night*

el nombre *name*
el norte *north*
novecientos(as) *nine hundred*
noventa *ninety*
noviembre *November*
nueve *nine*
nuevo(a) *new*
el número *number*

O

o *or*
el objetivo *objective*
el objeto *object*
obligatorio(a) *obligatory*
la oca *goose*
octubre *October*
ochenta *eighty*
ocho *eight*
ochocientos(as) *eight hundred*
la película del oeste *Western (film)*
el oeste *west*
el ojo *eye*
once *eleven*
la oportunidad *opportunity*
el orden *order*
el ordenador *computer*
ordenar *to put in order*
la oreja *ear*
el origen *origin*
original *original*
el oro *gold*
oscuro(a) *dark (colour)*
el otoño *autumn*
otro(a) *another, other*
los otros *the others, the rest*
la oveja *sheep*

P

el padre *father*
los padres *parents*
la página *page*
el país *country*
el País Vasco *Basque Country*
el pájaro *bird*
la palabra *word*
la paloma *dove, pigeon*
el pan *bread*
Panamá *Panama*
el pantalón *trousers*
el pantalón corto *shorts*
los (pantalones) vaqueros *jeans*
el papá *Dad*
el papel *paper*
Paquistán *Pakistan*
paquistaní *Pakistani*
para *for; in order to*
para beber *to (have to) drink*
para comer *to (have to) eat*
Paraguay *Paraguay*

el parchís *game played with counters*
la pared *wall*
el parque *park*
el paseo *avenue, boulevard*
el pasillo *hallway*
la pasta de dientes *toothpaste*
el pastel *cake*
la pastilla *pill*
la patata *potato*
las patatas fritas *chips; crisps*
patinar *to skate*
el patio *playground*
pedagógico(a) *educational*
peinarse *to brush one's hair*
el pelo *hair*
la película *film*
la pelota *ball; Spanish ball game*
pequeño(a) *small*
pero *but*
el perro *dog*
la persona *person (m/f)*
personal *personal*
la personalidad *personality*
Perú *Peru*
la peseta *peseta*
el pescado *fish (to eat)*
el pez *fish*
el piano *piano*
el pie *foot*
la pierna *leg*
el pijama *(m) pyjamas*
el ping-pong *table tennis*
el pino *pine tree*
pintar *to paint*
el pintor/la pintora *painter*
la pintura *painting (course)*
el pío *cheep, chirp*
la piragua *canoe*
la piscina *swimming pool*
el piso *flat (apartment); storey, floor*
el primer piso *first floor*
la pizarra *blackboard, whiteboard*
la pizza *pizza*
el plano *plan*
la planta *plant*
la planta baja *ground floor*
de plástico *plastic*
el plátano *banana*
el plato *plate*
la playa *beach*
la plaza *square (place)*
el plural *plural*
la película policiaca *thriller film*
el pollo *chicken*
popular *popular*
por *for*
por favor *please*
¿por qué? *why?*
porque *because*

la postal *postcard*
el póster *poster*
practicar *to practise*
la pradera *meadow*
el precio *price*
preferir *to prefer*
la pregunta *question*
preguntar *to ask a question*
el premio *prize*
preparar *to prepare*
presentar *to introduce someone*
presentarse *to introduce oneself*
la primavera *spring*
primero(a) *first*
el primo/la prima *cousin*
la princesa *princess*
principal *main*
el profesor/la profesora *teacher*
el programa *(m) programme*
la pronunciación *pronunciation*
pronunciar *to pronounce*
la proyección *showing (film)*
el proyecto *project*
el pueblo *small town, village*
la puerta *door*
Puerto Rico *Puerto Rico*
el puma *puma*
el punto *point*
en punto *exactly, precisely (time)*

Q

¿qué? *what?*
¿qué hora es? *what time is it?*
¿qué tal? *how are you?*
¿qué te pasa? *what's the matter?*
querer *to want*
querido(a) *dear*
el queso *cheese*
¿quién? *who?*
la química *chemistry*
quince *fifteen*
quinientos(as) *five hundred*
los quintillizos *quintuplets*

R

la radio *(f) radio*
el ratón *mouse*
real *royal*
el recreo *break, playtime*
recto(a) *straight*
rechazar *to reject*
el refresco *soft drink*
el regalo *gift*
la regla *ruler*
regular *so-so, all right*
la religión *religion*
el reloj *watch, clock*
repasar *to revise*
el repaso *revision*

repetir *to repeat*
República Dominicana *Dominican Republic*
responder *to reply*
el restaurante *restaurant*
el resultado *result*
el río *river*
el robot *robot*
la rodilla *knee*
rojo(a) *red*
romántico(a) *romantic*
la ropa *clothing, clothes*
la ropa interior *underwear*
rosa *pink*
el rotulador *felt-tip pen*
rubio(a) *blonde, fair (hair, skin)*
la rueda *circle; wheel*
el rugby *rugby*

S

el sábado *Saturday*
saber *to know (about something)*
el sacapuntas *pencil sharpener*
el saco de dormir *sleeping bag*
la sala *large room*
la sala de juegos *games room*
salir *to go out; leave*
el salón *living room, lounge*
saludar *to greet*
El Salvador *El Salvador*
la salchicha *sausage*
la sandalia *sandal*
las sandalias de agua *plastic sandals*
el sandwich *sandwich*
el sarrio *Pyrenean mountain goat*
seguir *to continue, follow*
el segundo *second (time)*
segundo(a) *second*
seis *six*
seiscientos(as) *six hundred*
la selección nacional *national team*
la semana *week*
el fin de semana *weekend*
señalar *to indicate*
septiembre *September*
ser *to be*
serio(a) *serious*
en serio *seriously*
los servicios *services; toilets*
sesenta *sixty*
la sesión *session*
setecientos(as) *seven hundred*
setenta *seventy*
si *if*
sí *yes*
la siesta *siesta*
siete *seven*
significar *to mean*
el signo *sign*
el silencio *silence*

en silencio *in silence*
la silla *chair*
el sillón *armchair*
el símbolo *symbol*
similar *similar, like*
simpático(a) *nice (person)*
sin *without*
sincero(a) *sincere*
singular *singular*
sobre *about; on (top of)*
sobre todo *especially, above all*
el sofá *sofa*
el sol *sun*
hace sol *it's sunny*
el sonido *noise, sound*
la sopa *soup*
la sopa de letras *word-search game*
su(s) *his, her, its*
subir *to go up, climb*
la subvención *grant, subsidy*
el suelo *floor; ground*
la suerte *luck*
la buena suerte *good luck*
la mala suerte *bad luck*
el supermercado *supermarket*
el sur *south*

T

el talento *talent*
el taller *workshop*
el taller de arte *art room*
el taller de manualidades *crafts workshop*
también *also, too*
tapar *to cover*
la tarde *afternoon*
de/por la tarde *in the afternoon*
buenas tardes *good afternoon/evening*
la tarea *chore, task*
la tarjeta *postcard*
el taxi *taxi*
la taza *cup*
el té *tea*
el teatro *theatre*
el teléfono *telephone*
la televisión *television*
la temperatura *temperature*
tener *to have*
tener bigote *to have a moustache*
tener gafas *to wear glasses*
el tenis *tennis*
el tenis de mesa *table tennis*
tercero(a) *third*
terminar *to finish*
el test *test*
el terror *horror*
la película de terror *horror film*
la tía *aunt*
el tiempo *time, weather*
el tiempo libre *free time*

la tienda *shop*
la tienda de camping *tent*
el tigre *tiger*
el tío *uncle*
típico(a) *typical*
el tipo *type*
tirar *to throw*
la tirita *plaster (for cut)*
tocar *to touch; play (an instrument)*
te toca *it's your turn*
todo(a) *all, everything*
todo recto *straight on*
todos los días *every day*
toma *here you are, take*
tomar *to take*
la tormenta *storm*
la tortilla *omelette*
la tortuga *tortoise*
la tostada *piece of toast*
el total *total*
en total *altogether, in total*
los trabajos manuales *handicrafts*
el trabalenguas *tongue-twister*
tradicional *traditional*
el traje *costume; suit*
el traje regional *regional costume*
la tranquilidad *peace, quiet*
trece *thirteen*
treinta *thirty*
el tren *train*
tres *three*
trescientos(as) *three hundred*
el trigo *wheat*
triste *sad*
tú *you*
tu(s) *your*
el turco *Turkish language*
turco(a) *Turkish*
Turquía *Turkey*
el turrón *almond-based sweet*

U

un *a, one (m)*
una *a, one (f)*
único(a) *only*
la unidad *unit*
el uniforme *uniform*
unir *to join, link*
la universidad *university*
uno *one (m)*
Uruguay *Uruguay*
usar *to use*

V

la vaca *cow*
las vacaciones *holidays*
de vacaciones *on holiday*
ir de vacaciones *to go on holiday*
vale *fine, OK*

los (pantalones) vaqueros *jeans*
vasco(a) *Basque*
el vaso *glass (for drinking)*
el vegetariano/la vegetariana *vegetarian*
veinte *twenty*
Venezuela *Venezuela*
venezolano(a) *Venezuelan*
venir *to come*
la ventana *window*
ver *to see, to watch*
ver la televisión *to watch television*
el verano *summer*
la verbena *open-air dance*
el verbo *verb*
verde *green*
la verdura *vegetables*
el vestido *dress*
vestirse *to get dressed*
la vez *time (occasion)*
a veces *sometimes*
el viaje *journey, trip*
la vida *life*
el vídeo *video*
la vídeo consola *video game*
el viento *wind*
hace viento *it's windy*
el viernes *Friday*
visitar *to visit*
la vista *view*
vivir *to live*
el vocabulario *vocabulary*
el/la vocalista *singer, vocalist (m/f)*
el voleibol *volleyball*

Y

y *and*
ya *now; already*
el yayo/la yaya *grandad/grandma*
yo *I*
el yogur *yoghurt*

Z

la zapatería *shoe shop*
las zapatillas de deporte *sports shoes, trainers*
el zapato *shoe*
la zona *area, zone*
el zumo *juice*
el zumo de naranja *orange juice*

A

a *un/una (m/f)*
about *sobre*
above all *sobre todo*
abroad *el extranjero*
to accept *aceptar*
accident *el accidente*
action *la acción*
activity *la actividad*
to adopt *adoptar*
address *la dirección*
adventure *la aventura*
adventurer *el aventurero/la aventurera*
advertisement *el anuncio*
afternoon *la tarde*
good afternoon *buenas tardes*
in the afternoon *de/por la tarde*
afterwards, then *después*
all, everything *todo*
all right, so-so *regular*
already, now *ya*
also, too *también*
altogether, in total *en total*
amongst, between *entre*
and *y (e before i and hi)*
angry *enfadado(a)*
animal *el animal*
anorak *el anorak*
another, other *otro(a)*
to answer *contestar*
apartment *el apartamento*
apple *la manzana*
approximately *aproximadamente*
April *abril*
Arab *el/la árabe*
Arabic *árabe*
architect *el arquitecto/la arquitecta*
architecture *la arquitectura*
area, zone *la zona*
Argentina *Argentina*
Argentinian *argentino(a)*
arm *el brazo*
armchair *el sillón*
to arrive *llegar*
art *el arte; el dibujo*
art room *el taller de arte*
article *el artículo*
to ask a question *preguntar*
athletics *el atletismo*
attention *la atención*
August *agosto*
aunt *la tía*
authentic *auténtico(a)*
automobile *el automóvil*
autumn *el otoño*
avenue *la avenida; el paseo*

B

baby *el bebé (m/f)*
backwards, behind *atrás*
bad; unwell *mal*
badminton *el bádminton*
bag *la bolsa*
school bag *la cartera*
sleeping bag *el saco de dormir*
toilet bag *la bolsa de aseo*
ball; Spanish ball game *la pelota*
ballpoint pen *el bolígrafo*
banana *el plátano*
bank *el banco*
baseball *el béisbol*
basketball *el baloncesto*
Basque *vasco*
Basque Country *el País Vasco, Euskadi*
Basque language *el euskera*
bass (musical instrument) *el bajo*
bath *el baño*
to bathe; have a bath *bañarse*
bathroom *el cuarto de baño*
to be *ser; estar*
beach *la playa*
beautiful *guapo(a)*
because *porque*
bed *la cama*
to go to bed *acostarse*
bedroom *el dormitorio*
bedside table *la mesilla*
beech tree *el haya (f)*
to begin, start with *empezar*
Bengali *bengalí*
behind *detrás (de); atrás*
below, underneath *debajo (de)*
beside, next to *al lado (de)*
best *el/la mejor (m/f)*
best friend *el mejor amigo*
between, amongst *entre*
bicycle *la bicicleta*
bidet *el bidé*
big *grande*
bilingual *bilingüe*
biology *la biología*
bird *el pájaro*
birthday *el cumpleaños*
happy birthday *feliz cumpleaños*
biscuit *la galleta*
black *negro(a)*
blackboard, whiteboard *la pizarra*
blonde, fair (hair, skin) *rubio(a)*
blouse *la blusa*
blue *azul*
body *el cuerpo*
Bolivia *Bolivia*
book *el libro*
bookshop *la librería*
boot *la bota*

Vocabulario

bored *aburrido(a)*
Bosnia *Bosnia*
Bosnian *bosnio(a)*
bottom *el fondo*
at the bottom (of) *al fondo (de)*
boulevard *el paseo*
box *la casilla*
boxing *el boxeo*
boy *el chico; el niño*
brand, make *la marca*
bread *el pan*
break, playtime *el recreo*
breakfast *el desayuno*
to have breakfast *desayunar*
brother *el hermano*
brothers (and sisters) *los hermanos*
brown *marrón*
to brush one's hair *peinarse*
building *el edificio*
bus *el autobús*
but *pero*
to buy *comprar*

C

café *la cafetería*
cake *el pastel*
calculator *la calculadora*
calendar *el calendario*
to be called *llamarse*
campsite; summer camp *el campamento*
Canary Islands *las islas Canarias*
canoe *la piragua*
cap, hat *la gorra; el gorro*
car *el coche*
card, form *la ficha*
playing cards *las cartas*
carnival *la carnaval*
fitted carpet *la moqueta*
to carry, wear *llevar*
cartoons *los dibujos animados*
cassette *el cassette*
Castilian Spanish *el castellano*
cat *el gato*
Catalan language *el catalán*
Catalonia *Cataluña*
to celebrate *celebrar*
centre *el centro*
cultural centre *el centro cultural*
town centre *el centro de la ciudad*
ceramics, pottery *la cerámica*
cereals *los cereales*
chair *la silla*
champion *el campeón/la campeona*
to change, exchange *cambiar*
chart, grid *el cuadro*
to check, compare *comprobar, comparar*
check pattern *de cuadros*
cheese *el queso*
chemist shop *la farmacia*

chemistry *la química*
chest of drawers *la cómoda*
chicken *el pollo*
for children *infantil*
Chile *Chile*
chimney *la chimenea*
China *China*
Chinese *chino(a)*
chips; crisps *las patatas fritas*
chocolate (drink/food) *el chocolate*
to choose *elegir*
chore, task *la tarea*
cinema *el cine*
city, large town *la ciudad*
class; classroom; type *la clase*
to clean *limpiar*
to clean one's teeth *lavarse los dientes*
to climb, go up *escalar, subir*
clinic *la clínica*
clock, watch *el reloj*
clothes, clothing *la ropa*
social club *el club*
clubs (cards) *los bastos*
coast *la costa*
coffee *el café*
coin *la moneda*
cold *frío(a)*
it's cold *hace frío*
colour *el color*
Columbia *Colombia*
Columbian *colombiano(a)*
to come *venir*
comfortable *cómodo(a)*
companion, classmate *el compañero/la compañera*
compare, check *comprobar, comparar*
compasses *el compás*
competition *la competición*
to complete *completar*
computer *el ordenador*
concert *el concierto*
constitution *la constitución*
to continue, follow *continuar, seguir*
cooker *la cocina*
cool *fresco(a)*
it's cool *hace fresco*
to correct *corregir*
correct *correcto(a)*
corridor, hallway *el pasillo*
Costa Rica *Costa Rica*
costume; suit *el traje*
regional costume *el traje regional*
swimming costume *el bañador*
country *el país*
countryside, field *el campo*
course of study *el curso*
cousin *el primo/la prima*
to cover *tapar*
cow *la vaca*
craft *la manualidad*

crafts workshop *el taller de manualidades*
crisps; chips *las patatas fritas*
to cross *cruzar*
crossword *el crucigrama (m)*
crow *la chova*
Cuba *Cuba*
Cuban *cubano(a)*
cultural *cultural*
cultural centre *el centro cultural*
cup *la taza*
cupboard; wardrobe *el armario*
curtain *la cortina*
cycling *el ciclismo*

D

Dad *el papá*
daily *diario(a)*
dance *la danza*
dancing *el baile*
to dance *bailar*
dark (colour) *oscuro(a)*
dark (hair, skin) *moreno(a)*
data *los datos*
database *la base de datos*
date *la fecha*
day *el día (m)*
every day *todos los días, cada día*
dear *querido(a)*
December *diciembre*
degree (temperature) *el grado*
to descend, go down *bajar*
to describe *describir*
to desire, wish for *desear*
description *la descripción*
to design *diseñar*
dialogue *el diálogo*
diary, notebook *la agenda*
dice (for game) *el dado*
to dictate *dictar*
dictionary *el diccionario*
difference *la diferencia*
different *diferente*
dining room *el comedor*
dinner; supper *la cena*
to have dinner/supper *cenar*
director *el director/la directora*
disco *la discoteca*
dislike *el disgusto*
to do, make *hacer*
doctor *el médico/la médica*
dog *el perro*
dollar *el dólar*
dolphin *el delfín*
Dominican Republic *República Dominicana*
donkey *el burro*
door *la puerta*
dove, pigeon *la paloma*
drama *el drama*
to draw *dibujar*
drawing *el dibujo*

dress *el vestido*
to dress, get dressed *vestirse*
to drink *beber*
drink *la bebida*
soft drink *el refresco*
drop (of liquid) *la gota*
drums *la batería*

E

each, every *cada*
eagle *el águila (f)*
ear *la oreja*
to earn, win *ganar*
east *el este*
to eat *comer*
Ecuador *Ecuador*
Ecuatorial Guinea *Guinea Ecuatorial*
education *la educación*
physical education *la educación física*
educational *pedagógico(a)*
eight *ocho*
eight hundred *ochocientos(as)*
eighteen *dieciocho*
eighty *ochenta*
elbow *el codo*
eleven *once*
El Salvador *El Salvador*
end (film) *el fin*
end (event) *el final*
at the end (of) *al final (de)*
England *Inglaterra*
English language *el inglés*
English *inglés/inglesa*
enjoyable, fun *divertido(a)*
enormous *enorme*
to enter *entrar*
entrance *la entrada*
entrance ticket *la entrada*
equipment; team *el equipo*
equivalent *equivalente*
eraser, rubber *la goma*
especially *sobre todo*
every, each *cada*
every day *todos los días, cada día*
everything *todo*
example *el ejemplo*
excellent *excelente*
exchange *el intercambio*
to exchange, change *cambiar*
excursion, trip *la excursión*
to go on an excursion *ir de excursión*
exercise (physical) *la gimnasia*
exercise (task) *el ejercicio*
exercise book *el cuaderno*
exhibition *la exposición*
to explain *explicar*
expression *la expresión*
eye *el ojo*

F

factory *la fábrica*
family *la familia*
family (adj) *familiar*
famous *famoso(a)*
fancy dress *el disfraz*
fantastic *fantástico(a)*
far (from) *lejos (de)*
fat *gordo(a)*
father *el padre*
favourite *favorito(a)*
February *febrero*
felt-tip pen *el rotulador*
festival, party *la fiesta*
field, countryside *el campo*
fifteen *quince*
fifty *cincuenta*
fillet *el filete*
film *la película*
to find *buscar, encontrar*
to finish *terminar*
fir tree *el abeto*
fireworks *los fuegos artificiales*
first *primero(a)*
fish *el pez; (to eat) el pescado*
five *cinco*
five hundred *quinientos(as)*
lemon fizzy drink *la gaseosa*
flag *la bandera*
flask *la cantimplora*
flat (to live) *el piso*
floor, ground *el suelo*
first floor *el primer piso*
ground floor *la planta baja*
flower *la flor*
to follow, continue *seguir, continuar*
food; meal *la comida*
foot *el pie*
football *el fútbol*
football stadium *el estadio de fútbol*
table football *el futbolín*
for, in order to *para*
for (time) *durante*
foreign *extranjero(a)*
foreigner *el extranjero/la extranjera*
form, card *la ficha*
forty *cuarenta*
fountain *la fuente*
four *cuatro*
four hundred *cuatrocientos(as)*
fourteen *catorce*
France *Francia*
free time *el tiempo libre*
freezer *el congelador*
French language *el francés*
French (adj) *francés/francesa*
Friday *el viernes*
fridge *el frigo*

friend *el amigo/la amiga*
sweet fritter *el churro*
from; since *desde*
in front of *delante (de)*
fruit *la fruta*
fun, enjoyable *divertido(a)*
in fun *en broma*
funfair *la feria*
furniture *los muebles*

G

Galicia *Galicia*
Galician Spanish *el gallego*
Galician *gallego(a)*
game *el juego*
festival game *la cucaña*
games room *la sala de juegos*
garden *el jardín*
geography *la geografía*
German *alemán/alemana*
German language *el alemán*
Germany *Alemania*
to get up *levantarse*
giant *el gigante*
gift *el regalo*
girl *la chica; la niña*
glass (for drinking) *la copa, el vaso*
glasses (spectacles) *las gafas*
to wear glasses *tener gafas*
to go *ir*
to go down, descend *bajar*
to go out *salir*
to go to bed *acostarse*
to go up, climb *subir, escalar*
goat *la cabra*
gold *el oro*
good; well *bueno(a)*
good afternoon/evening *buenas tardes*
good day/morning *buenos días*
good night *buenas noches*
goodbye *adiós*
goose *la oca*
grandad, grandpa *el abuelito/yayo*
grandfather *el abuelo*
grandma, granny *la abuelita/yaya*
grandmother *la abuela*
great, wonderful *estupendo(a)*
Greece *Grecia*
Greek language *el griego*
Greek *griego(a)*
green *verde*
to greet *saludar*
grey *gris*
grid, chart *el cuadro*
ground, floor *el suelo*
ground floor *la planta baja*
group *el grupo*
Guatemala *Guatemala*
to guess *adivinar*

guitar *la guitarra*
gymnasium *el gimnasio*
gymnastics, exercise *la gimnasia*

H

hair *el pelo*
to brush one's hair *peinarse*
hallway *la entrada, el pasillo*
hamburger *la hamburguesa*
hand *la mano (f)*
handball *el balonmano*
handicrafts *los trabajos manuales*
happy *contento(a), feliz*
happy birthday *feliz cumpleaños*
hat, cap *la gorra; el gorro*
to have *tener*
here you are, take this *toma*
he *él*
head *la cabeza*
headache *el dolor de cabeza*
heart *el corazón*
heat *el calor*
hello *hola*
it's hot *hace calor*
height *la estatura*
to help *ayudar*
here *aquí*
high, tall *alto(a)*
his, her, its *su(s)*
history; story *la historia*
hockey *el hockey*
roller hockey *el hockey patines*
holidays *las vacaciones*
on holiday *de vacaciones*
to go on holiday *ir de vacaciones*
home, house *la casa*
at home *en casa*
homework *los deberes*
Honduras *Honduras*
horror (adj) *de terror*
horror film *una película de terror*
horse *el caballo*
hospital *el hospital*
it's hot *hace calor*
hotel *el hotel*
hour *la hora*
house, home *la casa*
how are you? *¿qué tal?*
how is it spelt? *¿cómo se escribe?*
how many? *¿cuántos(as)?*
how much is it? *¿cuánto es?*
how? what? *¿cómo?*
hug *el abrazo*
hundred *cien*
one hundred *ciento*
hurt *el dolor*
to hurt *doler*

I

I *yo*
ice cream *el helado*
ice hockey *el hockey patines*
ideal *ideal*
identical *igual*
if *si*
ill *enfermo(a)*
to imagine *imaginar*
important *importante*
in *en*
in order to, for *para*
to include *incluir*
to indicate *indicar, señalar*
to indicate, mark *marcar*
individually *individualmente*
information *la información*
information technology *la informática*
instruction *la instrucción*
interesting *interesante*
interview *la entrevista*
to introduce oneself *presentarse*
to introduce someone *presentar*
to invent *inventar*
invitation *la invitación*
to invite *invitar a*
Ireland *Irlanda*
Irish *irlandés/irlandesa*
island *la isla*
Italian *italiano(a)*
Italian language *el italiano*
Italy *Italia*

J

jacket *la chaqueta*
Jamaica *Jamaica*
Jamaican *jamaicano(a)*
January *enero*
jeans *los (pantalones) vaqueros*
job, work *el trabajo*
to join, link *unir*
joke *el chiste*
journey, trip *el viaje*
judo *el judo*
juice *el zumo*
orange juice *el zumo de naranja*
July *julio*
jumper, sweater *el jersey*
June *junio*

K

kitchen; cooker *la cocina*
knee *la rodilla*
knickers *la braga*
to know (something) *saber*

L

laboratory *el laboratorio*
to lack, be missing *faltar*
lamp *la lámpara*
language *el idioma, la lengua, el lenguaje*
to last *durar*
later *luego*
see you later/soon *hasta luego*
Latin America *Latinoamérica*
Latin American *latinoamericano(a)*
laundry *la lavandería*
to learn *aprender*
to leave *salir*
left (direction) *la izquierda*
on/to the left *a la izquierda*
leg *la pierna*
lemon *el limón*
lemonade *la gaseosa*
letter *la carta*
letter (of alphabet) *la letra*
library *la biblioteca*
life *la vida*
like, similar to *como*
to like *gustar*
like *el gusto*
list *la lista*
to listen *escuchar*
to listen to music *escuchar música*
literature *la literatura*
a little *un poco*
to live *vivir*
living room, lounge *el salón*
long *largo(a)*
to look at *mirar*
to look for *buscar*
lottery *la lotería*
lounge, living room *el salón*
love from (in letter) *un abrazo*
lots of love (in letter) *un abrazo fuerte*
luck *la suerte*
good luck *la buena suerte*
bad luck *la mala suerte*

M

main *principal*
to make, do *hacer*
make, brand *la marca*
make-up *el maquillaje*
manner *la manera*
map *el mapa (m)*
March *marzo*
to mark, indicate *marcar*
mathematics *las matemáticas*
what's the matter? *¿qué te pasa?*
May *mayo*
meadow *la pradera*
meal; food *la comida*
to mean *significar*

meat *la carne*
memory *la memoria*
menu *el menú*
metal (adj) *de metal*
metre *el metro*
Mexican *mexicano(a)*
Mexico *México*
milk *la leche*
milkshake *el batido*
to mime *mimar*
mineral water *el agua mineral (f)*
minute *el minuto*
mirror *el espejo*
to be missing, lack *faltar*
mistake *el error*
modern *moderno(a)*
Monday *el lunes*
money *el dinero*
monitor, supervisor *el monitor/la monitora*
monkey *el mono*
monster *el monstruo*
month *el mes*
monument *el monumento*
more, most *más*
morning *la mañana*
in the morning *de/por la mañana*
most *más*
mother *la madre*
mountain *la montaña*
Pyrenean mountain goat *el sarrio*
moustache *el bigote*
to have a moustache *tener bigote*
mouse *el ratón*
mouth *la boca*
Mum *la mamá*
museum *el museo*
music *la música*
to listen to music *escuchar música*
my *mi(s)*

N

name *el nombre*
what's your name? *¿cómo te llamas?*
national *nacional*
nationality *la nacionalidad*
natural sciences *las ciencias naturales*
near (to) *cerca (de)*
necessary *necesario(a)*
to need *necesitar*
niether ... nor ... *ni ... no ...*
new *nuevo(a)*
next to *al lado (de)*
Nicaragua *Nicaragua*
nice (person) *simpático(a)*
night *la noche*
good night *buenas noches*
nine *nueve*
nine hundred *novecientos(as)*
nineteen *diecinueve*

ninety *noventa*
no; not *no*
noise, sound *el sonido el ruido*
north *el norte*
nose *la nariz*
not; no *no*
note (money) *el billete*
notebook, diary *la agenda*
November *noviembre*
now *ahora*
number *el número*

O

object *el objeto*
objective *el objetivo*
obligatory *obligatorio(a)*
occasion, time *la vez*
occasionally, sometimes *a veces*
occupation *la profesión*
October *octubre*
of, about, from *de*
older *mayor*
omelette *la tortilla*
on, about *sobre*
on, at *en*
on time, exactly *en punto*
on top (of) *encima (de)*
one *uno/una (m/f)*
one o'clock *la una*
two o'clock *las dos*
only *único(a)*
to open *abrir*
opportunity *la oportunidad*
opposite *enfrente (de)*
or *o*
orange *la naranja*
orange (adj) *naranja*
orange juice *el zumo de naranja*
order *el orden*
in order to *para*
put in order *ordenar*
origin *el origen*
original *original*
other *otro(a)*
the others *los demás*
to go out *salir*
overcoat *el abrigo*
overseas *el extranjero*

P

page *la página*
pain *el dolor*
to paint *pintar*
painter *el pintor/la pintora*
painting *la pintura (course)*
Pakistan *Paquistán*
Pakistani *paquistaní*
Panama *Panamá*
paper *el papel*

Paraguay *Paraguay*
parents *los padres*
park *el parque*
party; festival *la fiesta*
peace, quiet *la tranquilidad*
ballpoint pen *el bolígrafo*
pencil *el lapicero*
pencil case *el estuche*
pencil sharpener *el sacapuntas*
people *la gente*
person *la persona (m/f)*
personal *personal*
personality *la personalidad*
Peru *Perú*
peseta *la peseta*
pharmacy *la farmacia*
Philippines *las Filipinas*
photograph *la foto*
photography *la fotografía*
physical education *la educación física*
piano *el piano*
picture; grid, chart *el cuadro*
pig; pork *el cerdo*
pill *la pastilla*
pink *rosa*
pine tree *el pino*
pizza *la pizza*
place *el lugar*
plan *el plano*
plant *la planta*
plaster (for cut) *la tirita*
plastic (adj) *de plástico*
plate *el plato*
to play (game) *jugar*
to play (instrument) *tocar*
playground *el patio*
playing cards *las cartas*
playtime, break *el recreo*
please *por favor*
plural *plural*
point *el punto*
swimming pool *la piscina*
popular *popular*
pork; pig *el cerdo*
postcard *la postal, la tarjeta*
poster *el póster*
potato *la patata*
pottery, ceramics *la cerámica*
pound sterling *la libra esterlina*
to practise *practicar*
to prefer *preferir*
to prepare *preparar*
pretty *bonito(a)*
price *el precio*
princess *la princesa*
prize *el premio*
street procession *el desfile*
programme *el programa (m)*
project *el proyecto*

to pronounce *pronunciar*
pronunciation *la pronunciación*
Puerto Rico *Puerto Rico*
puma *el puma*
pyjamas *el pijama (m)*

Q

quarter *el cuarto*
quarterpounder (hamburger) *el cuarto de libra*
question *la pregunta*
to ask a question *preguntar*
quintuplets *los quintillizos*

R

rabbit *el conejo*
race *la carrera*
radio *la radio (f)*
to rain *llover*
it's raining *llueve*
to read *leer*
red *rojo(a)*
regional *regional*
regional costume *el traje regional*
to reject *rechazar*
to relax, rest *descansar*
religion *la religión*
to repeat *repetir*
to reply *responder*
to rest, relax *descansar*
the rest *los demás*
restaurant *el restaurante*
result *el resultado*
to revise *repasar*
revision *el repaso*
right (direction) *la derecha*
on/to the right *a la derecha*
river *el río*
robot *el robot*
roller hockey *el hockey patines*
romantic *romántico(a)*
room *el cuarto, la habitación*
large room *la sala*
royal *real*
rubber, eraser *la goma*
rucksack *la mochila*
rug *la alfombra*
rugby *el rugby*
ruler *la regla*

S

sad *triste*
salad *la ensalada*
sandal *la sandalia*
plastic sandals *las sandalias de agua*
sandwich *el sandwich*
crusty bread sandwich *el bocadillo*
Saturday *el sábado*
sausage *la salchicha*
to say, tell *decir*

scarf *la bufanda*
scatterbrained *cascabelero(a)*
school *el colegio, la escuela*
school bag *la cartera*
school subject *la asignatura*
science *las ciencias*
natural sciences *las ciencias naturales*
social sciences *las ciencias sociales*
science fiction *la ciencia ficción*
Scotland *Escocia*
Scottish *escocés/escocesa*
sea *el/la mar (m/f)*
season; station *la estación*
second (time) *el segundo*
second *segundo(a)*
to see, watch *ver*
see you soon/later *hasta luego*
self-evaluation *la autoevaluación*
to send *enviar, mandar*
sentence *la frase*
September *septiembre*
serious *serio(a)*
seriously *en serio*
service *el servicio*
session *la sesión*
seven *siete*
seven hundred *setecientos(as)*
seventeen *diecisiete*
seventy *setenta*
shampoo *el champú*
she *ella*
sheep *la oveja*
shelf *la estantería*
shell *la concha*
shirt *la camisa*
shoe *el zapato*
shoe shop *la zapatería*
sports shoes, trainers *las zapatillas de deporte*
shop *la tienda*
shop assistant *el dependiente/la dependienta*
short *bajo(a)*
shorts *el pantalón corto*
shower *la ducha*
to shower *ducharse*
side *el lado*
be side, next to *al lado (de)*
siesta *la siesta*
sign *el signo*
silence *el silencio*
in silence *en silencio*
similar, like *similar*
since, from *desde*
sincere *sincero(a)*
to sing *cantar*
singer *el/la cantante (m/f), el/la vocalista (m/f)*
singular *singular*
sink *el fregadero(kitchen); el lavabo*
sister *la hermana*
six *seis*

six hundred *seiscientos(as)*
sixteen *dieciséis*
sixty *sesenta*
to skate *patinar*
skateboard *el monopatín*
skeleton *el esqueleto*
skiing *el esquí*
to ski *esquiar*
skill *la destreza*
skirt *la falda*
to sleep *dormir*
sleeping bag *el saco de dormir*
slim *delgado(a)*
slow(ly) *despacio*
small *pequeño(a)*
afternoon snack *la merienda*
to have an
afternoon snack *merendar*
snow *la nieve*
to snow *nevar*
it's snowing *nieva*
soap *el jabón*
social sciences *las ciencias sociales*
sock *el calcetín*
sofa *el sofá*
soft drink *el refresco*
sometimes *a veces*
song *la canción*
so-so, all right *regular*
sound, noise *el sonido, el ruido*
soup *la sopa*
south *el sur*
space *el espacio*
spaghetti *los espaguetis*
Spain *España*
Spanish language *el español*
Spanish (adj) *español/española*
spark *la chispa*
to speak, talk *hablar*
spectacles, glasses *las gafas*
to spell *escribir*
how is it spelt? *¿cómo se escribe?*
sport *el deporte*
sports shoes, trainers *las zapatillas de deporte*
spring *la primavera*
square (place) *la plaza*
stadium *el estadio*
football stadium *el estadio de fútbol*
stairs *la escalera*
start, begin *empezar*
station; season *la estación*
storm *la tormenta*
story; history *la historia*
storey, floor *el piso*
first storey *el primer piso*
straight *recto(a)*
straight on *todo recto*
strawberry *la fresa*
street *la calle*

street procession *el desfile*
strong *fuerte*
student *el/la estudiante (m/f)*
to study *estudiar*
school subject *la asignatura*
suit; costume *el traje*
summer *el verano*
summer camp *el campamento*
sun *el sol*
it's sunny *hace sol*
Sunday *el domingo*
sunmat *la esterilla*
suntan lotion *el bronceador*
supermarket *el supermercado*
supervisor, monitor *el monitor/la monitora*
supper; dinner *la cena*
to have supper/dinner *cenar*
survey *la encuesta*
sweater, jumper *el jersey*
to swim *nadar*
swimming *la natación*
swimming costume/trunks *el bañador*
swimming pool *la piscina*
sword *la espada*
symbol *el símbolo*

T

tape *la cinta*
table *la mesa*
table football *el futbolín*
table tennis *el ping-pong, el tenis de mesa*
to take *tomar*
take this *toma*
talent *el talento*
to talk, speak *hablar*
tall *alto(a)*
task, chore *la tarea*
task, exercise *el ejercicio, la actividad*
taxi *el taxi*
tea *el té*
teacher *el profesor/la profesora*
team *el equipo*
national team *la selección nacional*
telephone *el teléfono*
television *la televisión*
to watch television *ver la televisión*
to tell, say *decir*
temperature *la temperatura*
ten *diez*
tennis *el tenis*
table tennis *el ping-pong, el tenis de mesa*
tent *la tienda (de camping)*
test *el test*
thank you *gracias*
the (f) *la*
the (m) *el*
theatre *el teatro*
then, afterwards *después*
there is/are *hay*

these *estos(as)*
they *ellos/ellas*
thin *delgado(a)*
thing *la cosa*
third *tercero(a)*
thirteen *trece*
thirty *treinta*
this *éste, ésta, esto*
thousand *mil*
three *tres*
three hundred *trescientos(as)*
thriller film *la película policiaca*
throat *la garganta*
to throw *tirar*
Thursday *el jueves*
ticket (bus, train) *el billete*
entrance ticket *la entrada*
to tidy up *arreglar*
tiger *el tigre*
tights *las medias*
time (clock) *la hora*
time, occasion *la vez*
time (period); weather *el tiempo*
free time *el tiempo libre*
what time is it? *¿qué hora es?*
timetable *el horario*
tired *cansado(a)*
piece of toast *la tostada*
today *hoy*
toilets *los servicios*
toilet bag *la bolsa de aseo*
tomorrow *mañana*
tongue *la lengua*
tongue-twister *el trabalenguas*
too, also *también*
tooth *el diente*
toothbrush *el cepillo de dientes*
toothpaste *la pasta de dientes*
on top (of) *encima (de), sobre*
torch *la linterna*
tortoise *la tortuga*
total *el total*
in total *en total*
to touch *tocar*
large town, city *la ciudad*
small town, village *el pueblo*
toy *el juguete*
track suit *el chándal*
traditional *tradicional*
train *el tren*
trainers, sports shoes *las zapatillas de deporte*
tree *el árbol*
trip, excursion *la excursión*
to go on a trip *ir de excursión*
trip, journey *el viaje*
trousers *el pantalón*
swimming trunks *el bañador*
T-shirt; vest *la camiseta*
Tuesday *el martes*

Turkey *Turquía*
Turkish *turco(a)*
twelve *doce*
twenty *veinte*
two *dos*
two hundred *doscientos(as)*
type *la clase, el tipo*
typical *típico(a)*

U

ugly *feo(a)*
uncle *el tío*
underneath, below *debajo (de)*
underpants *los calzonzillos*
underwear *la ropa interior*
uniform *el uniforme*
unit *la unidad*
university *la universidad*
until *hasta*
unhappy; unwell *mal*
United States *los Estados Unidos*
Uruguay *el Uruguay*
to use *usar*

V

vegetables *la verdura*
vegetarian *el vegetariano/la vegetariana*
Venezuela *Venezuela*
Venezuelan *venezolano(a)*
verb *el verbo*
vest; T-shirt *la camiseta*
video *el vídeo*
video game *la vídeo consola*
view *la vista*
village, small town *el pueblo*
to visit *visitar*
vocabulary *el vocabulario*
vocalist, singer *el/la vocalista (m/f)*
volleyball *el voleibol*
vulture *el buitre*

W

to wait *esperar*
to wake up *despertarse*
Wales *Gales*
wall *la pared*
to want *querer*
war *la guerra*
war (adj) *de guerra*
war film *la película de guerra*
wardrobe *el armario*
to wash *lavar*
to wash oneself *lavarse*
watch *el reloj*
to watch television *ver la televisión*
water *el agua (f)*
mineral water *el agua mineral (f)*
in this way *así*
we *nosotros(as)*

to wear, carry *llevar*
to wear glasses *tener gafas*
weather; time *el tiempo*
Wednesday *el miércoles*
week *la semana*
weekend *el fin de semana*
well; good *bien*
Welsh *galés/galesa*
west *el oeste*
Western (film) *la película del oeste*
what? how? *¿cómo?*
what's it like? *¿cómo es?*
what's the matter? *¿qué te pasa?*
what's your name? *¿cómo te llamas?*
what time is it? *¿qué hora es?*
what? *¿qué?*
wheat *el trigo*
when *cuando*
when? *¿cuándo?*
where? *¿dónde?*
where (to)? *¿adónde?*
which? *¿cuál?*
white *blanco(a)*
whiteboard, blackboard *la pizarra*
who? *¿quién?*
why? *¿por qué?*
win, earn *ganar*
wind *el viento*
it's windy *hace viento*
window *la ventana*
winter *el invierno*
to wish for, desire *desear*
witch *la bruja*
with *con*
with me *conmigo*
with you *contigo*
without *sin*
wonderful, great *estupendo(a)*
wood (with trees) *el bosque*
word *la palabra*
word-search game *la sopa de letras*
work, job *el trabajo*
workshop *el taller*
crafts workshop *el taller de manualidades*
world (adj) *mundial*
world *el mundo*
to write *escribir*

Y

year *el año*
yellow *amarillo(a)*
yes *sí*
yoghurt *el yogur*
you (informal) *tú (sing), vosotros(as) (plur)*
you (formal) *usted (sing), ustedes (plur)*
for young people *juvenil*
younger *menor*
your *tu(s)*

Z

zero *cero*
zone, area *la zona*